CW01668492

Ski In Control: How to ski ANY piste, anywhere, in full control.

Ski In Control: How to ski ANY piste, anywhere, in full control.

Man or Woman Young or Old

Bob Trueman

VALENTINE TRUEMAN PUBLISHING

Contents

Introduction

Dear Reader,

The vast majority of ski instructors, and the industry itself, believe the way to improve your skiing is just to keep being told what to do, be shown demonstrations, and then do it. I don't. If it were true there would be more expert skiers about. Yet there are very few despite the fact that we ALL have the potential. And I believe that includes you.

What is it that isn't working? What is missing? Essentially two things; firstly help in handling our minds , and secondly a true *understanding* of what makes skiing work. Without those foundations mostly what happens is a bit disappointing; good enough fun but not as satisfying as we would like.

If you are the sort of person who prefers to get on with the physical aspects first, and you want to know what skiing is and how it works, go straight to chapter 14 and read on from there, because skiing is almost certainly not what you think it is. (A clue: it is *not* about sliding around on snow). Amazing though that may appear.

But I am going to suggest that you will short-change your self if you do not then come back and read from the beginning, because what matters most is what happens in our minds, and the first two thirds of the book address what you can do about that. Any degree to which our skiing is held back, isn't caused by a physical inability to make the simple movements required (you could make those when you were two years old), it is caused by our thinking, and by our mis-perceptions of how skiing happens, and by our emotions. Jumping across a three-foot gap at ground level is easy, but we find it scary if the gap is a 1000 ft drop. It's the same gap.

Why is skiing difficult?

The answer is simple: lack of friction. In almost every instant of our lives, day-to-day, minute-to-minute our functioning, even survival, depend upon friction.

We couldn't walk across the floor without it. We couldn't bring our car to a stop at the traffic lights without it. We certainly couldn't walk down a slope without it. Even sitting on this chair, as I am, would be impossible; the slightest movement would deposit me on the floor only to stop when I hit the wall.

And yet we choose to go skiing despite, perhaps even because the activity is to all intents and purposes friction-less.

An alien not having seen it done might surmise that it must be impossible. And yet it clearly is. So something other than friction must be in play.

This book examines and explains in simple terms why it is possible, and how to do it. Or if you are already a skier, how to do it better.

The ski world is full of glossily produced books, replete with perfect photographs of marvellous skiers, all sold on the basis that if you see a perfect picture of a perfect skier you will be able to do some perfect skiing. I don't believe that. This book of mine has a few simple photographs often of home-made artifacts included as aids to the much more important words. It has one picture of a skier.

It is ideas and understandings that help you to become an expert skier, not pictures, or demonstrations by an expert. What really makes the difference is what you think, what you do, and what you **feel.** Not what you see.

You can make bigger changes to your skiing sitting on a park bench and thinking, than you can by looking at too many pictures, or indeed by "getting the miles in" while you increasingly embed bad habits. Your imagination is of more use to you than your eyeballs, and anyway park benches are pleasant places to spend an hour or two.

Ski school does not seem to work very well at producing expert skiers, and most people give up ski schools after a while with a sense of disappointment. Some traipse around following "guides" but that seems no more effective at developing increased mastery.

Some skiers have no interest in becoming skillful, they are quite happy just to ski about no matter how well or how poorly. And that is perfectly fine. Others want to enjoy the satisfaction of exercising a degree of mastery of the sport. You are the ones I'm after!

Progress for a lot of folk is halted by trepidation and the strangeness of skiing being possible at all. After spending fifty one weeks on a horizontal high-friction surface the experience of spending a week standing on two artifacts deliberately designed to be slippy, on an inclined surface with almost no friction, is something wondrous. And a little disconcerting.

But we know that skiing can be done, and we know it can be done in difficult terrain. We know it can be done by humans, and we know that humans all have similar brains even if they are used differently. So skiing, *always in full control on ANY piste, and with justifiable confidence that it will go well,* ought to be possible for us, too. I assure you, it is.

This is not a perfect book, it has some layout errors, but if I wait for perfection it will never get published. I wrote it to give you hope, and to do that by explaining what ski schools don't have time to explain, and most instructors don't know anyway: namely how skiing works and what it is; and why there is every reason to believe you could do it very well.

Nowhere do I suggest it is easy – there's not much satisfaction in easy – everywhere do I explain that it is simple and predictable if you're taught correctly. It takes practice – has to be good practice – but if "she" can do it, so can you. Young or old, man or woman.

There are additional FREE papers on my blog, and on my website where you will also find my email should you wish to write to me. My website is http://www.bobski.com My email is bobski@bobski.com couldn't be simpler.

Bob Trueman.

1.

Chapter 1: A message of hope for ALL skiers.

I recently came across a quotation by Mahatma Ghandi –

"Your beliefs become your thoughts
Your thoughts become your words
Your words become your actions
Your actions become your habits
Your habits become your destiny"
Ghandi

It took me years to realise that you will never develop skillful controlled skiing – or anything else physical – by watching an expert do it, or looking at pictures of experts doing it.

There is a little known but significant difference between "instructing", as offered in a ski-school environment, and "coaching". Each has its place. The primary purpose of ski schools is to look-after, entertain, and help beginner skiers to enjoy their holiday and go from non-skiers to skiers who can navigate easy slopes reasonably safely. Based on a commercial logic, by and large it has not proved to be a model which takes skiers on to mastery of the sport.

Coaching is sport based. It can easily take six years to qualify as a coach, sometimes more. There are far fewer coaches than instructors. Coaches are not allowed to teach complete beginners. Coaching implies longer term relationships and a very different teaching delivery method that relies on delivering understandings more than on visual demonstrations. Coaching essentially says that advanced skiing is learned by guided understanding rather than attempting to copy demonstrations by a good skier. International competitors are coached.

Ghandi's observation may seem at first a little high-falutin' for a book on skiing, but all of my experience as a coach proves that it is fundamental to changing your skiing. Let's work our way back up it from the bottom.

We each of us have a way in which we ski. Good, bad or indifferent that's what we've got. The kind of skiing we presently do has *become* our skiing destiny. It is that way because of the habits we have developed both physical and mental – the things we do, the way we do them and what we think, about skiing and about ourselves.

We express our thoughts in words for the most part, sometimes enunciated to others, sometimes just inside our heads. And our thoughts about skiing are encapsulated in our beliefs both about the activity itself, and perhaps more importantly about our selves. Oftentimes they can be unjustifiably limiting self beliefs.

Anybody can become a skilled, controlled skier. Anybody. It is nonsense to suppose that only “born athletes” (there is no such thing) can do it. The potential to become a first rate skier does not suddenly atrophy when you get to forty. Neither is it closed off to you if you are born female, nor if you’re not young. Anybody can do it and it is never too late. What you need is a better style of teaching and learning than most people get access to.

I was persuaded to put my ideas about skiing into a small book because I have coached (not instructed) skiers for some decades now and I’m happy to say have had hundreds of successes and only two or three failures. I define “success” by a pupil discovering they really could bring about a level of skiing skill they didn’t think was possible for them before they studied with me.

Much later in the book I will give you plenty of practical things you can do when you’ve got your skis on. For the time being I’m going to ask you to be patient, and be willing to address the many other aspects of learning, coaching and skiing, which take up more of the book’s space than the simple exercises.

I’m asking you this for a number of reasons. Firstly, there are plenty of books with pictures of how you ‘ought’ to ski, what to do ”in the bumps”, how to “handle powder”, and so forth. Plenty of references to “angulation” (now known to be a false and sometimes dangerous suggestion); no shortage of people telling you to separate your upper body from your lower body – an idea with good intent but a rather poor way of expressing it.

Secondly, what matters most is what you *feel* and what it means when you feel it. I call that “The Kneed to “Knowtice”, explained later. That requires considerable understanding of the *processes* that work best, not just the outcomes you’d like, and a much better knowledge and understanding of the interaction between the ski and the snow, as you ski . You won’t need to spend as much time on it as a coach does, but all the learning you can grab will be more than worth the effort.

“Ski In Control”™ synthesises decades of experience in helping capable enough, but often rather disappointed skiers to overcome previously insurmountable hurdles put in their way by their earlier instruction, (or lack of instruction) to their becoming the skillful controlled skiers they always wanted to be; not necessarily super-fast and wild, but feeling happy to be skillful and precise; to always ski in control on ANY piste anywhere, any conditions.

I pondered long on whether or not I should search for a "writing style" for the book, but in the end I decided just to be me, because that seems to have been what has worked best for my hundreds of pupils over the years. So while at times it may be a trifle quirky, I hope it will be enjoyably readable. Mostly I hope it helps you to change your skiing to more of what you want.

It is clear that for very many skiers, the way you have been taught has done little more than get you down slopes somehow, usually with not too much damage, but with little predictability, even less grace, and a slight sense of disappointment sometimes. Going home after your week's skiing no better than you were last year. I have been surprised by the number of my adult, experienced pupils who were still rather unsure why, when success does occur, it has occurred. It's hard to attribute the success to ourselves if we are unsure how it came about.

When we first begin skiing our rate of learning and improvement is retarded by "The Three Horrible Hurdles":

1. **Bewilderment** (what's happening? Why did it/didn't it happen, and so on?)

2. **Apprehension** (what will happen if I cannot control this?)

3. And **self-denigration** through internal monologues like describing our experiences to ourselves as "hopeless", "not good enough", "I ought to be better than this by now", and a whole lot more.

Recognizing that people want to "get skiing", the "instruction" method of teaching in ski schools jumps immediately to an exhortation to "follow me, and do what I do". In my view that is jumping the gun. I understand why it happens, and I think it is inevitable. It will get you started but it is not a method which will in the end enable you to become a skillful all-terrain skier. Nor will just "getting the miles in".

I want this book to help those people who want to ski a great deal better than they have done so far. My teaching is aimed at –

- cutting out bewilderment by enabling you to learn what makes skiing happen (Isaac Newton knew a thing or two about it),
- by minimising apprehension, through the use of the simplest practice techniques in the most appropriate terrain,
- and by continuously working with you to help you change the

internal monologues that may well have been holding you back without your realising it.

Having goals like "must ski a red run by Thursday, and a black run before I go home" is not conducive to skill development and tends to put a cap on long term performance, often referred to as "the plateau". Although it has to be said we can use them for short term motivation.

That type of goal does not work well as a method of learning much and can easily lead to ingrained habits which hold you back. What is needed is a three-fold approach:

1. **Preparation** – without proper preparation the mental strengths that will underpin your physical experiments and trials will be missing, and everything you physically do to change your skiing, will be on shaky ground.

2. **Comprehension** – because that is what learning is, and without it fear can build up quite needlessly. It is impossible to learn something you do not understand, or when you are scared.

3. **Execution** – this is the phase in which you "do things" and go out and experiment.

Miss out the first two, and rely only on the last one, and your progress will be very quickly halted. You will end up on "the plateau". You may ask yourself, when was the last time you successfully brought about a desired change in something you did not understand? I never did.

Let me tell you what this ski book is not.

Most skiing books of my acquaintance are replete with photographs of the author, or some racer, skiing wonderfully. My skiing is not wonderful, but it is good enough to support what I hope is better teaching, so "Ski In Control™" does not contain any pictures of me .

You cannot learn much by looking at pictures, or watching someone else, **especially** if they are expert. You can get a general impression. No more. By how much can you improve your tennis by watching Roger Federer? As often as not, watching someone else skiing wonderfully just depressed me; perhaps you found the same? Words are more important because our minds control our bodies, not the other way round, and it is by words that we communicate our experience of our universe.

Now let me tell you what it is.

This book is just a tool-kit. It is a work book. Some skiers are interested in what they ski, (How many miles have we done today? Did we tick-off all the pistes? Can we "ski the resort out by Tuesday! (I wonder what that means?). But other skiers are more interested in *how* they ski. They just want to ski *well*. This book is aimed at those who care how they ski and want to improve it.

It is aimed primarily at adult skiers, but not exclusively so. It is a book of hope and encouragement. Learn to use what is in here and you will become a skillful skier no matter your age or gender. Becoming skillful at skiing does not demand that you must be very young, very fit, or very glamorous. I am indeed the proof! Healthy and motivated will suffice.

Most of my pupils have been middle aged or more. Almost all of them (over 97%) have transformed their skiing far beyond their expectations; and so can you. Almost all of them initially had regrettably – and quite unjustifiably – low levels of self-expectation where their skiing had been concerned. Many commented later on how what we did together helped them in other areas of their lives.

The typical initial self-view has been that "it's too late to get any good", or "if only I'd started younger", or "I'll never be as good as that skier over there" and so on. With only a tiny number of exceptions they have all with me achieved massive improvements in their skiing; changes in their levels of self-belief; big improvements in their self-confidence and tremendous satisfaction from their extra skiing skill.

I distill decades of successful coaching of healthy folk but not fitness-fanatics; of the middle-aged and older, and of people with inquisitive, lively, often well-educated minds. It has been an unmitigated pleasure. My pupils have mostly been people who ski recreationally (plus a few instructors and aspirant coaches). They have been almost exactly evenly divided between men and women; folk who always wanted to get better but had not managed to find the best method until we introduced them, on our courses, to the understandings and techniques that I explain in this book.

If you visit bobski.com you can see from my pupils' comments that the processes I will show you brought them to levels of skillfulness and confident control in their skiing which previously they had never dreamed they could ever achieve. Some told me after their first week with me that they had been on the very verge of giving up skiing until committing to these ideas and processes. Many of them now spend a lot of their skiing time in the off-piste. No small number are now better skiers than me.

"Crumpled by the long-continued ill-usage to which they have been subjected".

I am reminded of the observation by the respected geologist, Henry M Cadell, who described certain rocks as "crumpled by the long-continued ill-usage to which they have been subjected".

Almost all my pupils have skied for a considerable number of years, most have attended numerous ski schools in various countries, and been disappointed that the teaching they received did not in the end help them develop their skiing as far as they had hoped. They never got the feeling of control and mastery they longed for. Most of them ended up blaming themselves for their lack of skiing development, (boy, have I been there!) when they should have blamed the system that was meant to help them improve, but didn't.

I maintain that you have every right to believe that you can be a truly skilful skier; competent and controlled. If you are not one already, never think that those who are, are in some way better than you, they just learned differently. You can do it. If you have not already done it, then you have not learned in the best environment. Never believe you are "past it".

Again, I am the proof. I started skiing in middle age! Skiing was never a natural process for me, I had to work at it. I was slow. I was actually told repeatedly for eight years, by what I now know to be poor teachers (often they were excellent skiers) that I would never be any good. They were wrong. I had potential. So do you.

Eventually I stumbled upon a first rate coach, Gerald Harrison, who in just a week helped me to transform my skiing trajectory. He helped me change my limiting self-beliefs; my trust in myself. He gave me hope! I cannot thank him enough for that.

I want to do the same for you.

I did not instantly become a brilliant skier, far from it, (actually the truth is I never became a brilliant skier!) but I subsequently, after a lot of very enjoyable "work", became an international alpine skiing coach and some time back-country skier, because he helped me to believe I could. I have met, been taught by, and worked with a few really good skiing teachers. They are not in abundant supply.

If you want to win races or free-ride events you will need to be young, super fit, very athletic, gymnastic, fearless, or all of those. To be a skillful, controlled skier you just need to want to be. The key requirements are desire, guidance, and persistence. Olympic coach Frank Dick used to say "you only need to want it, work at it, and persist".

To ski with more control and more enjoyment all you need is a better learning process, which is what this book and my courses are intended to show you. It isn't easy. It isn't instantaneous, but it is simple, and eminently possible. You can do it, and it is hugely satisfying.

My book and my courses are ways in which I hope to open the door to the pleasure and satisfaction that my own (very few great) teachers made available to me. I hope they work for you. Good luck with your efforts. Perhaps we'll meet on a slope somewhere. I hope so.

Bob Trueman.

2.

Chapter 2: No Tricks, just process.

Understanding makes the difference

"The fox has many tricks. The hedgehog only one. But that is the best of all."

Desiderius Erasmus (1466-1536)

There is no "magic trick" you can buy that will help your skiing instantly improve. The idea is quite a seductive one but it is wrong. Equally the idea that someone who is a World Cup winner will be a better teacher for you is false. They got paid for their skiing, not their teaching abilities. How *they* ski is immaterial. Those ideas lead you up the garden path, not effectively down the piste.

It is akin to the idea that if someone else shows you a perfect demonstration, you should be able to emulate it. Frustrating isn't it, when you can't?

Instructors could demonstrate until they were blue in the face, but for 8 years my skiing didn't change materially as a result. Eventually I realised that watching someone else, especially if they were expert, isn't what works. If we could learn by watching, I could be a concert pianist. I've seen Ashkenazy do it – it looked easy!

So when I set out to write this book, I had very much in mind that we need to find something else, something that is missing from other books; something that has been missing from the more usual teaching. In the end, and using my own (haltingly erratic) skiing development as my guide, I finally realised what it was.

The real breakthrough came when I began to understand two things – firstly how to learn; and secondly how the results I was actually getting, came into being; why my skiing results were the way they were. After that, I found the Confidence, the Control of my mind, the Concentration and the Commitment to try new things, new approaches, new ideas; to test them out, and not be disappointed when some of them did not immediately work. I learned how to learn something worthwhile from every experiment I conducted.

This book has a sequenced structure, but it may well be best not to just start at the beginning and work your way through to the end. For some that may prove to be less efficient from a learning viewpoint than "hopping about" through the book. It depends on how you learn. Everybody is different, and if you have found that what works for you best is indeed to methodically work through from beginning to end, then do that. All I want is for this book to be a successful resource for you. I want it to help you really make changes to your skiing. It is just a toolkit.

Try using a technique from Accelerated Learning – have a look through the chapter headings and then take a quick overview of anything that immediately catches your eye. Your subconscious already knows what will be most appropriate for you. Trust it, and go there first.

Then, skim read some of the other chapters. Fly over the book and get a bird's eye view; it will help you get a better perspective on it and get more out of it later on.

Finally, go again to the ones which first caught your eye and read them thoroughly. If there are any suggested things to do in there, do them as you go along. It has been absolutely proven that we forget nearly everything we are told, and most of what we read, but we remember most of what we do, so I really do recommend that you do any exercises and practices.

Change? Who needs change, things are bad enough already!"

The core that runs through this book like copper wire through an electric cable is change. That's what you want to do. You want to stop doing what you do at the moment, or the way you do it, and to do something different, so that you *get* something different. Albert Einstein is usually credited with having defined madness as the process of continually doing the same thing while expecting a changed outcome.

Our context happens to be skiing, but it could equally well be tiddly-winks, high level management, trout fishing, learning to be a master chef or anything else. My goal for this book is that it should help you to find new ways to change your mind, and your skiing. I want you to "change your mind, and keep the change". The single most important requirement for the development of skilful skiing is for you to have self-confidence, and a belief that you could achieve your skiing goals if only you could find the right way of going about it.

Well you can. It is possible. That applies no matter your age, no matter if you are a man or a woman, 70 years old or 35. Self-confidence and fear are on the two ends of a continuum. Neither of them is given to you from outside, both are generated by us ourselves, internally. We do this using cues we pick up from the world around us. What matters is what we do with those cues.

William Shakespeare wrote *"Nothing is either good or bad, but thinking makes it so"*. This is an important theme in this book.

Psychologist Susan Jeffers PhD says there is only one kind of fear. It is often differently dressed but is always the same. The fear is – "I may not be able to 'handle' this; (whatever the current 'this' is) and I don't know what the outcome might be if I can't". We cannot learn while we are afraid. Our fear may be anything from physical injury to mere embarrassment, or something as nebulous as "letting ourselves down". In all cases it will inhibit your learning.

Self confidence is self-generated; gradually.

Self-confidence has to be self-generated because it can come from nowhere else. We must take charge of our selves. Very few folk have ever been shown how to go about it, and this book goes some way to correct this. I hope.

Self-confidence cannot be generated in great big leaps; it can only be done in small carefully designed steps. Every one of us needs the same thing, none of us is any different. We need to move forward a small increment at a time, then to embed it soundly until we know before we do it next time that we have every reason to believe that "we *will* be able to handle it". Only then should we move on to the next small increment. Being impatient will set you back, and slow you down. There are some "white papers" on **www.bobski.com** about this.

As more and more successes are aggregated the process speeds up, and you become a much more self-confident person. You have created a virtuous circle that builds and builds. If there is anything in here that you would like to discuss further, or some aspect you come across that you would like to expand upon, or do not fully understand, then visit, **www.bobski.com** or email me at **bobski@bobski.com** and I will be glad to help you in any way that I can. I will welcome your feedback.

One more thing – I found that it was learning how learning itself happens, and the chain of elements that brings about results, which really enabled me to change my own skiing. It was understandings that did it. I was not a born skier and I doubt there is such a thing. It was akin to the old adage that "If you give a man a fish you feed him for a day. Teach him how to fish, you feed him for a lifetime".

This new way of looking at the problem enabled me to become an international skiing coach at a fairly advanced age, having been "stalled" for years in ordinary ski school situations, or on plastic slopes and the like. There is nothing special or spectacular about me. If I can do it, you can do it.

I think it was Phil Smith who once said to me that "everybody loves skiing, but the ones who do it the best, love it the most".

You can be one of them.

3.

Chapter 3: Fifty weeks of practice every year

Opportunity knocks: most folk don't hear it.

Most folk go skiing for one or two weeks a year. We want to get the most out of those two weeks. Most folk also do no preparation for their skiing trip, waiting instead until they get on the slope for the first time since last year before putting their boots in the bindings and putting their minds to it.

Small wonder then that many of us approach the first day with a mixture of anticipated pleasure diluted by considerable trepidation. It need not be like that.

Every year presents you with about fifty weeks away from the slopes, during which you can do a vast amount of very pleasurable "work" on your skiing. Not physical effort, unless you choose to visit an artificial slope regularly but instead, mind games that really work, and that you can even play in bed if you want to.

There is so much you can do away from the slopes that will set you up immensely well for the time when you actually are on the snow.

There is a story, quite true, of a competitor who seriously injured herself in practice – I think it was Picabo Street – and spent five months on her back recovering, unable to ski. Before her event she got back on the practice slopes with less than a month to go but still won the Gold Medal at the World Championships.

Asked how on earth she did it with no practice to help her, she apparently said "No practice? C'mon, I've lain on my back for five months and done eighteen hours of practice every day. I've had more practice than anyone else!" That was because she had spent years training herself how to imagine herself skiing.

You can use that approach. In later chapters I show you how to do it. You do not have to be an Olympic competitor; I will show you some of the mental techniques they employ and you can choose to practice them. Or not. Your choice. "Human beings get good at what they do".

I once asked Eddie (The Eagle) Edwards if he and the other jumpers really did use mental imagery (imagining) techniques. He looked amazed that I had asked and said “We never do anything else; I’m even “jumping” while I’m driving to the event. It’s a wonder I don’t crash the car”.

Michaelangelo and David

The story goes that after Michaelangelo sculpted the greatest work of art known to sculpting the Pope asked him how he did it. The great artist apparently said “It was easy; I just removed everything that wasn’t David”. Bit of a smarty-pants, Mike was.

But there is a philosophical school of thought based on precisely that idea – we can make significant progress by knowing and eliminating anything extraneous or disadvantageous.

There are just a few, but extremely important issues in skiing, which, if you eliminate them will make life not only easier but simpler, safer, and your skill development much more secure.

Many of these are ideas that have been implanted by either earlier instruction, or maybe a lack of instruction. Skiing is not an intuitive activity, our minds are not naturally designed to facilitate what works in skiing. Skiing is counter intuitive. What makes it work is the opposite of what your mind usually tells you.

Here are some things you must remove in order to bring out the exquisite ‘David’ in you :

- Straight legs
- Stiff legs
- Arms tucked into your body
- Standing up straight, or
- Sitting back with your ankles at right-angles and your weight being supported by the strength of your thigh muscles.

Just half a dozen simple things. Not too many to remember but too many to remember at the same time. Fortunately, one at a time will do. To get rid of those, what works is having something else to do instead. I will show you some.

You have the potential to be what you want to be.

After the Americans had put a man on the moon for the first time an over-excited and hyperbolic journalist asked the project leader how they had done this miracle. He replied that it was not a miracle; it was just something they had decided to do.

You could simply decide to be a more controlled and skilful skier. Don't treat it as an option; tell your "self "- "Listen! This is what we're going to do together, you and I. I've made up my mind!." It is an extraordinary fact, but true, that every movement you need to make in order to do controlled skilful skiing, you could make by the time you were just two years old. Landing on the moon didn't happen automatically and neither will controlled skiing, but both can be done.

The whole of the first section of this book is intended to help you prepare for making your skiing a great deal more effective, more controlled and much more satisfying for you.

A lot of this section is concerned with helping you to gain confidence in the fact – and it is a fact – that you really do have the potential to become the kind of skier you would like to be. You already have within you all the resources you need to bring about all of the changes you want. But you will need to do it. You don't get much for nothing. You will need to decide that you jolly well will make those changes happen.

MY GUARANTEE TO YOU

I will offer you a rock-solid, cast-iron, snow-proof, mahogany-lined, copper sheathed, no-small-print, A1-at-Lloyds guarantee, that if you choose to follow the processes in this book and do the "work" required, whether along with a good coach (which might well speed things up – especially when it comes to "carving", of which more later – much later), or even on your own, you will be able to transform your skiing and the enjoyment you get from it.

You can become a skier who skis in control on any piste, anywhere. Don't be put off by seeing young heroes and heroines skiing the half-pipe at the Olympics, and telling yourself "I'll never be like that, so I'll never be any good".

If you are amongst the many who are "on the plateau" then that is caused by two things. Firstly, you may not yet properly understand what is going on when skis do what they do. Few do. Secondly you have not yet been helped to creatively change what you have been doing, to take you nearer to where you want your skiing to be.

Now’s your chance.

4.

Chapter 4: Understanding beats trying too hard.

The Importance of Understanding

"Furious activity is no substitute for understanding"
H.H.Williams

I was in exactly that situation – stuck on the plateau – for eight solid years, trying hard, and then trying harder, and making no real progress at all. Like Homer Simpson said *"Mmm, trying; the first step on the road to failure!"* I tried throwing myself down steeper and steeper pistes in the stupid belief that this surely must make me change for the better. It didn't. All it did was scare me. And hurt sometimes.

Every year I turned up for my ski school, and by the end of the week, while I had admittedly had a good time, all I ever managed to do was to get back to the level I had been at, by the end of the same week, last year! It was like a recurring dream.

I was even taking lessons at a dry slope three times a week and yet my progress was absolutely minimal. Some instructors said that this was my fault. They were wrong, it was the teaching process. I proved this by using a different method and becoming an international skiing coach.

"When was the last time you succeeded at something you didn't really understand?"

Over the years it has become crystal clear that it is when my pupils get to *understand* skiing, that they first begin to make their great leaps forward. That is the time when their belief in themselves and in their own potential changes.

Every year we're really keen to get better, but no one has helped us to try a new route toward the destination. No one has helped us to create our own map of our ski universe, so we keep on trying to use someone else's, even though we know it has not brought any great changes in all the years we have been trying. If it's the only map you have, what choice have you got? When all you have is a hammer, everything looks like a nail.

When I was getting nowhere – and desperately wanted to improve – I started to blame myself. I started to believe that there was something wrong with me: that in some way I just wasn't cut out to be a skier; that in some way the good skiers I saw had been born that way and I hadn't.

There was no shortage of instructors at the dry slope ready to reinforce that wrong belief. It made them look better. It was depressing. It turned out not be true in my case, and it isn't true in yours.

Just skiing about won't help you improve, it just embeds habits you'd be better off without. And ski schools won't get you far either.

This book

– Helps you to learn how to learn

– Explains both how and why skis do what they do.

– Is likely to challenge some assumptions which instruction has led you to hold (I hope you'll be willing to try new things – to remake your world.)

– Uses modern sports coaching to give you simple ways to change (not necessarily easy, but simple) and enhance your ability, and your performance.

– Introduces ideas on how to control your own mind to eliminate blocks to progress.

– Helps you to learn how to "coach" yourself.

– And gives you some simple tasks you can incorporate into your own skiing which will help you develop a sounder, more secure and altogether more effective technique, for more-controlled skiing.

– **A key "take-away"**

– *If you always do what you have always done, you will always get what you always got. If it isn't working, do something else, anything else, no matter what.*

(And I don't mean give up skiing!).

Keep doing the same thing because nobody shows you an alternative possibility, and the result is likely to be dissatisfaction, the loss of hope, and often self-denigration.

Now imagine that someone comes along and says "Why don't you stop trying hard, and simply do something different instead? Try another route. Turn left sometime instead of right, even if you don't know where it leads to".

Imagine you do this, and you find yourself even further away from your goal. THIS IS A BRILLIANT RESULT! You tried something new. You got a result. That result told you something – it suggested the right direction simply by manifestly being itself the wrong direction. A wonderful, successful, positive result. Change, already.

It is this kind of willingness to experiment and try different things that eventually leads to real, and really effective, changes. By far the most beneficial changes in just about everything that has made our lives better over the millennia has been the result, not of academic introspection but rather experimentation and 'tinkering'; keeping what worked better, and throwing out what didn't.

Wheelwrights have fantastic specialised tools for their work, and amazing techniques; neither was developed in a classroom, they just made wheels that fell apart, and tinkered until they made wheels that didn't. The only thing that coaching does is to shorten the tinkering process – all the other claims are baloney. Tinkering with a purpose! Skillful tinkering.

There is a real danger that we will just conclude that we'll never make it; that we're not like the good skiers, and we learn to live with it. More time is spent in restaurants and we convince ourselves that all we really wanted was to cover as much ground as possible, no matter how clumsily. Perhaps our skiing will improve "with time" we think. It doesn't. It gets to feel more comfortable to us – our habits becoming our destiny – and we interpret that as improvement. This is one of those dreadful self-fulfilling prophecies we hear about. And it is so self-destructive. It is also – **wrong.**

I give you my word – it does not have to be like that. How do I know this? I know because I have been there. I got held back just as you are probably being held back.

You *can* become the skier you want to be. I have since proved it with too many folk for there to be any remaining doubt. You don't have to be young. You don't have to be male. You don't have to be super fit. You don't have to be particularly athletic. You may have to be patient. You may find you need to develop "stickability". But you can do it.

If you would like to be a better skier, you just need the book, and maybe some coaching. I am not saying it is easy. I am not suggesting it is necessarily quick, there are few shortcuts to anywhere worth going, but it is essentially simple. And it can be certain.

If you are bothering to read this book, then you are one of the determined ones and. . . . . you will succeed.

Coaching is essentially different from "instructing". There is too much to go into here, but suffice to say that under 'instruction' the job is for you to watch the instructor, so that you will be able, supposedly, to see what she does and copy it. In coaching it's our job to watch you do the skiing, and help you to develop an ability to interpret the feedback you get. We don't learn by watching, we learn by doing, and understanding what we are doing.

Coaching is better for those skiers who have found great pleasure in skiing but not enough progress, and who feel that somewhere inside them there still lies the potential to develop themselves much further.

They are correct in that. When you come onto the slope, you bring with you everything you need in order to bring about the changes you desire. Coaching is for people who want to express themselves more fully through skiing; for folk with a real desire to become skillful **in-control** skiers.

5.

Chapter 5: Why we get the results we do.

Here's why you get what you get.
(Or the 1 – 2 – 3 – 4 of life.).

"If you always do what you've always done, you'll always get what you've always got"

A Neuro Linguistic Programming observation.

Why do you get what you get? Why does what actually happens, happen? Sometimes we get a result we want and sometimes we don't. Sometimes we have no control over what we get, but usually, somewhere along the line, what we are getting has been brought about by our own actions, or decisions. Or at the very least by the way in which we have responded to a circumstance.

Certainly this is the case in our chosen sport of skiing. Whatever the outcome, desirable or otherwise, we are responsible. If I lose control in a 45° couloir and slide half a mile to the bottom, breaking most of my bits in the process, the responsibility is mine – either because I applied a less than optimal technique, or perhaps because my original decision to enter the thing in the first place was not wise: I wasn't up to it. Bad judgement.

Neuro Linguistic Programmers and others have created a model for understanding why we get the outcomes we do, and while it is criticised by some as incomplete, I have found it helped me, and certainly helps my pupils, to redirect our efforts to bring about changes that work. Change is inherently difficult and we need all the help we can get with it.

Getting what we get is a four-step process, and it is like digging down to deeper levels to find the foundations,
it goes like this:-

Level 1 ("Ground Level") : THE OUTCOME

Let us say that something happens. Your ski either does what you want, exactly how you want it, or it does not, and perhaps you don't know why. Nevertheless, like it or not, you achieved an outcome. A result, desirable or otherwise.

Where did this result come from? It wasn't sent by the Gods. It was not mere chance. Something, perhaps some combination of things, caused it. Buddhists say that there is nothing without a cause. Not even a rebel.

Let's say the event was that your ski lost grip. Let's say further, that your ski often loses grip. The question then is, why does your ski do what it does? The answer that tells us the most; the one which best helps us to construct a method or a process that will help us learn in the future, and helps us to learn how to learn, is this –

"Our outcomes result from our behaviours"

"Behaviours" is the psychologists' fancy term for "what we actually *do*". So put simply, what we do governs what we get. Which is all very well, but why do we do what we do ? This leads us to the next level down.

Level 2 ("The first basement") : BEHAVIOURS

We now have an outcome, and we know that this resulted from what we did. The new question is why was that what we did? Where do behaviours themselves come from; why are the behaviours the way they are? Why did we not do something else?

Just like outcomes, behaviours have causes. If outcomes result from behaviours; what do behaviours result from?

Behaviours result from our thinking.

Level 3 ("The sub-Basement") : THINKING

Behaviours have their genesis in thinking. What we do is born from what we think; how we think; and when we think it. Born of our "cognitions".

We do what we do, for example pivoting the ski; or rotating our shoulders, or whatever it may be, because of our thinking around the situation in which we do these things. (These particular things by the way are two things better avoided !).

The only way we humans can direct our physiques to carry out an action, is by having gone through a thought process prior to that action, and then having our brains direct our physiques to carry out the action.

So everything I do is the result of some combination of what I think, how I think, and possibly when I think it. Normally in our daily lives this process goes on subconsciously; I don't have to consciously think of what to do in order to pick up a coffee cup and put it to my lips; it is a ready-practiced programme that runs automatically. In a skiing context, it could go like this :

1. I want to change direction.
2. I think about how that might be achieved. I may not be aware that I'm thinking this, but subconsciously I most certainly am, and quite possibly consciously.
3. Let's say that at the the time it seems to me to be logical that to change direction, I will need to change the direction my ski is pointing.
4. So I work out how to pivot my foot, in order to twist the ski into a new direction, and that is what I do.

But what if, in this imagined scenario, neither I, nor the ski, do in fact make the directional change I am looking for. What if all that happens is that I keep going in the same direction, only now with the ski turned across its direction of travel instead of pointing along it. Cognitive dissonance occurs – I feel confused.

Or perhaps it did change direction but clumsily, insufficiently, with a general feeling of instability and unpredictability. I got an outcome, but it was not entirely the outcome I wanted, even though I changed my behaviours. So something perhaps was wrong with my thinking. – That after all directed my behaviours.

This begs the next question, and leads on to step 4, in our sequence.

Our thinking is constrained and directed by our beliefs.

Level 4 ("The Foundations"): OUR BELIEFS.

Our thinking can only be done within the framework of our belief systems. Our beliefs about our world and our existence are the box inside of which we think. They are the map; they are not the territory itself. They are not – at any rate not necessarily – the truth; they are only our perceptions.

In the case outlined thus far, I hope you can see that as I skied along, what happened was the outcome of what I did – and what I did was a resultant of what I thought. What I thought was controlled by my beliefs.

A long time ago someone told me in a loud voice to "turn your skis". That person was in a position of apparent knowledge and authority so I acted on their instruction. On that occasion I may have changed direction. But I didn't understand why. There will have been more than one cause. However, because at the time I did not understand all the aspects of the process, my belief became that – "if I wish to change direction I must 'turn' my skis".

Once that became my belief, it governed all my thinking, which governed all my actions which delivered my results for a very long time thereafter, even though the result I got was a mystery to me, and not particularly good. ("Turn your skis" by the way is a rather poor instruction, of which more later!) It became habituated.

This 1-2-3-4 process applies to everything in our lives, but you may by now have recognized how it can lead us up the garden path. What we come to believe may not be real or the truth, or especially may not be all the truth, but only a part of it. So we can see that our belief may be no more than merely a perception and a faulty one at that.

Unfortunately, once we have a belief, and until we can learn and understand enough of our subject to change that belief, it will continue to direct our thinking, our actions, and deliver up our outcomes. This is why the opening phrase of this chapter is so powerful – "If you always do what you've always done, you will always get what you always got". You won't get far by trying to just change what you do, and short-cutting steps two, three, and four.

Henry Ford is reputed to have said – "Whether you believe you can or you can't, you're right". Beliefs are deep-seated and oft-times sub-conscious.

Later I will expose the four worst instructions you have ever had – and you will be able to see how, because of the circumstances at the time you were given them, they perhaps became part of your belief system about skiing. And because of that, they may well have contributed to the stagnation of your skiing development.

If no one helps you to change your perceptions, your thinking, and your beliefs about skiing you will be consigned to the never ending plateau of no improvement, and only be able to keep on trying the same old things, which you have already established only partially work, if they work at all. Worse than that, by constantly repeating them you embed them more deeply as a natural habit and make them even more difficult to shift.

For the time being I want to ask you just to hold on to this thought –

What you *believe*, directs and constrains your *thinking*.
Your *thinking* is what directs your *behaviours* (what you do)
Your *behaviours* are what produce your *outcomes*.

The main implication of this observation for your skiing , is that your current skiing is the way it is because of your beliefs – conscious or otherwise – about what you need to do in order to get the ski to do what you want; modified perhaps by beliefs about yourself. And not least of course by how much skiing you've managed to do, and what kind of teaching and help you've had.

In order to change, we need to work on those beliefs. Stay with me, and we will do just that.

6.

Chapter 6: The most important six inches in skiing.

Skiing's most important six inches.

"She can do it when she puts her mind to it"
"I'll do it when I have a mind to"
"I can't do it, it's doin' me 'ead in".

We have scores of phrases like this that we use every day. The reason is that we have a natural understanding of the importance of the mind. The importance of your mental "state" simply cannot be exaggerated.

Your skis may be anything from 150 to 210 centimetres long. Your boots will be around 30 cm along the sole. Your ski poles will be around 110 cm give or take. But the most important six inches in skiing is the six inches between your ears. If we don't change them, we won't change anything.

It isn't our feet, or our arms or our legs that inhibit our skiing progress – it's our minds. You can actually make all the movements you need to make in order to ski well, by the time you are two years old. Those movements are simple, and small. They are simple to do, but far from easy on sloping snow. To really improve your skiing you don't need to learn any new physical movements, you need to find how to make old ones in a "risk" situation.

Motivation

To be truly effective, before we start actually doing something we need to be motivated and we need to have a lot of information and understanding. For both of these you need your mind not your legs. I think the human mind has unlimited potential, but we have to know how to harness it. It does not come with an instruction book, that is why sport psychology and Accelerated Learning are so important.

I want to sell you on the idea of choosing to use your mind to change your skiing. Skiers who best change their *thinking* are the ones who change their *skiing* best; not the ones who believe that "practice makes perfect". Only perfect practice makes perfect. **All** practice makes permanent, so it is absolutely crucial that we are careful not to practice anything inappropriate or ineffective. We will simply get good at it. Hence my suggesting that you don't just "try harder" – all you will do is more deeply ingrain some things you already do and which are not working too well.

I have an idea that it is this 'thinking' requirement which is often missing when ski school lessons are taken. I am not disparaging the instructors, but from my own memories of attending ski schools, I can now recognise that while I was always trying to do the best I could, somehow my mind wasn't engaged. Perhaps it has something to do with not being the person with the responsibility; I was just there to do as I was told. My physical self was there, but I wasn't helped to learn how to learn, how to increase my awareness, or to find control of my mental processes.

I was most certainly not helped to become effective in the far from easy task of bringing about change. Change is difficult for most of us, so in a context such as skiing – which is done in challenging circumstances, learning how to do it becomes increasingly important, and decreasingly easy.

The Human Brain

The human brain is reputed to comprise some 100 billion neurons. Each of these is capable of developing twenty dendrites (little hairy extensions). Each dendrite is capable of connecting with other dendrites. The following piece of information nearly blew my socks off when I first came across it, and has been a major influence on me ever since – There are more potential neurological pathways in a human brain than there are atoms in the universe! (How do I know? I counted them!)

With this kind of potential, all you need to do to achieve anything you want, and certainly to improve your skiing, is to find some ways to harness it. And you can. The ways are not complex. Again, not easy but simple.

The Four "C's"

Practitioners of Sport Psychology have developed four groupings, which seriously affect and indeed control performance. The order shown here does not denote relative levels of importance.

- Commitment
- Confidence (self)
- Control (of self)
- Concentration.

And to these I want to add another one which umpteen decades of ski coaching have shown me is crucial to helping my pupils develop a new self-confidence, and that is –

- Understanding.

I'll be expanding on these as we go on but for the time being I just want to re-iterate that everything is possible for you. You have the inbuilt ability, once you use the right tools, to hugely increase your commitment, your self-confidence, your self-control, and your concentration. There is absolutely no doubt that you can become the kind of skier you always wanted to be.

Of course, there will prove to be some limits (I'm bumping into mine increasingly, it's called old age) but those limits will be WAY beyond what you might currently imagine. Just take a look at some of these actual comments from pupils about their potential. You can see many more on www.bobski.com

"…. My objective to ski confidently through technical competence was achieved half way through ….."
"…. You gave me a framework to understand how skis work and how to use them …."
" …. We got into the dark recesses of the shed at the back of my head, and found all the relevant tools required . . . "
"…. I feel much more confident now ….."
"… Really pleased with this new awareness I've got …."
"… I feel I will now be able to progress even further …."
"…. Felt good about myself, never demoralised …."

These extracts are from letters sent to me by folk who, prior to being introduced to the "mind tools" I am referring to, lacked self-confidence, lacked a belief in their own skiing potential, lacked a deep sense of commitment, and most certainly had never been helped to understand why skis do what they do, and how to get them to do it. Rather, they had come merely in hope.

By finding, and then using the tools that are available to help gain control of our own minds, all of those skiers, and many others too, have been able to change all these things Their self-belief and self-confidence. Their recognition of their real potential. Their ability to "hang in there" during temporary setbacks. Their skill with self-control techniques. And their ability to concentrate on the tasks in hand when skiing

These new abilities are underpinned by their new understandings. I said above that I wanted to "sell" you on the idea of using your mind to change your skiing. I hope I have done that. You can certainly do it; you can change your skiing. It's perhaps not too much of a claim to say that it can change your life. Some have said that.

I hope to lead you on a journey of understanding during which you will find it easier and easier to do the simple things, make the simple "movements in motion" as John Shedden calls them, which will transform you into the skillful skier you want to be. Gerald Harrison told me "simple, is best". My own skiing journey proved him right.

The best places to become good at doing the simple things are gentle slopes, at gentle speeds. Once you are good there, then that is the time to take them higher and steeper.

Some key "take-aways"

We have proved that your learning curve is steepest when the slope isn't.

We have proved that you learn faster when you ski slower.

We have proved that impatience keeps you waiting.

7.

Chapter 7: HOW to learn.

Learning. And *how* to learn skiing or anything else.

You don't absolutely *have* to read this chapter right now if you don't want to. But, in the longer term it is one of the more important chapters in the book.

It is not directly related to the practical "doing" things part of improving your skiing. However, you might want to come back to it at some stage because it certainly underpins learning itself, and puts everything you do in a context that will make change that much easier. Anything that does that simply has to be a Good Thing.

It is well worth learning how learning comes about. At school, and later at university, they don't teach you how to learn, they just assume that we all know, and that if information is put before us, then we will learn it. As usual, it is a case of "yes, and no". One thing is certain, and that is that it is perfectly possible to accelerate your learning rate, and to make the learning less problematical and more permanent.

You cannot see learning happening. All you can do is deduce that learning has occurred when you see some relatively permanent change in behaviour. Behaviour notice, not just understanding: that is to say, you begin **doing** something differently and relatively consistently.

There is a significant difference between understanding about something, and really understanding it. How many times have you thought you knew something and then when you tried to tell someone else, or answer an exam paper, you found you didn't really understand it at all? That was probably because you had read it, or heard it and remembered it, but you hadn't **done** it.

"Humans get good at what they do". So be careful what you do! This is another way of saying that practice makes permanent, not necessarily perfect.

If you become aware of a series of relatively permanent beneficial changes, however small they may be – and that is important, *however* small they may be – then you will be able to know that an on-going learning process is under way.

You may think as you read this next bit that it is "obvious", or "common sense", but often things are not obvious until after they have been pointed out; and the one attribute of common sense I have regularly observed, is that it isn't common.

When you have learned something, then by definition you know it. When you know it, it is not confusing – because you know it. You do not have to remember something you "know". When there is something you do not know, and are not trying to learn, you will not be confused, because you are not even thinking about it.

Confusion is not a Bad Thing. It is a Good Thing.

So confusion is almost a synonym for learning. If you are focused on something, and confused, then be encouraged because that means learning is happening. Not confused? Then either you already know it, or you're not learning it! Let's relate this to your skiing.

Bear with me, there is a reason for this next 'tale'. Many years ago during some training I had to do, we had to learn to fire a rifle. Accurately. For the course I was on it was imperative it was done well. On our first visit to the range we were given a rifle and ten rounds to shoot at one target. I put a lot of thought and effort into what I was doing, but when we went to collect our targets I found I had not got even one round inside the target's rings. All the holes were in the top right hand corner of the square card.

My nil score gave the attendant sergeant yet another excuse to vent his spleen on someone. Me. And yet my shooting had been very consistent, and therefore in one sense very good. How can that be? I missed the target but every round fell within a three inch circle, which in one way is excellent. (Much later, this consistency was added to by the requisite feedback and it proved rather useful.)

My *inputs* had been consistent and accurate. But the *outcome* had been useless. Why? Because I had not been able to see where my rounds had been landing, so all I could do was fire, and hope. There was no point in changing what I was doing because I had no feedback mechanism from the results of what I was doing, to guide any changes I might have wrought. Had I changed there was an equal probability that I would make matters worse, as make them better.

No comprehensible feedback = no learning.

It is the same with your skiing. You need to know exactly what you are trying to achieve, on that run, or even just on one part of a run, and you need to have a mechanism you can use to assess whether or not you get it. Only this *feedback* can guide what else you might try if you don't at first achieve your goal. The two most important elements in this process are (1) to know what your desired outcome is, and (2) then to know precisely *what* you are *getting*.

A key "take-away".

No feedback = no progress, other than by luck.

If you are aware of finding it difficult to make sense of what is happening under your skis, (in other words it's confusing) then that is excellent; not only are you clearly in the midst of your learning process, but better yet, you are *aware* of it. And awareness, if you are a skier, is Nirvana!

Even not knowing what is happening is a good result if you *know* that you don't know. What is useless for you is not knowing, and not knowing you don't know. (Yes, I know I'm beginning to sound like Donald Rumsfeld but go over it again and you'll see what I mean). It is precisely this which renders most ski school teaching so ineffective for developing any level of advanced skiing. You need a better model if you really want to become an expert.

You can identify four stages in learning something.

1. **Stage One – Unconscious Incompetence**, when we either do not know something or cannot do something, and what is more we don't even know we can't. I can remember skiing instructors telling me I was doing something or other inappropriate, and I didn't have the faintest idea that I was. I spent years thinking I could ski well, when all the time I did not have a clue! (I live in constant fear of that still being the case!)

2. **Stage two – Conscious Incompetence**, when we have become sufficiently aware and knowledgeable at least to know our limitations. We now know that we are less than fully competent. We become aware of what's happening. You need a certain degree of mental resilience at this stage to withstand the knock this gives your self-image. At this stage

you can easily become de-motivated. This is the stage where we find ourselves saying negative things to our selves – "I'm never going to be any good"; "I thought I was getting o.k., and now look at me!" Things like that. We need to summon up our resilience and self-believe at this point.

3. **Stage three – Conscious Competence**. We work at it, get better at it, and understand it enough to know that now at last we are developing competentence at it. By now we are beginning to feel better about our selves.

4. **Stage four – Unconscious Competence**. When we are truly expert we can do some things without conscious thought. Think back now on how many miles you drive in the car without needing to be constantly consciously aware of what you are doing, how to do it, or when. It just happens.

This four-stage process occurs whenever you are learning something, no matter what that something is. It is accompanied by a variety of changing emotions. In the absence of knowing this, those emotions can become very troublesome, indeed distressing. But once you know about this process their power over you diminishes. You can identify what stage you have got to, and will feel natural.

When you are in a learning state, you should be confused. You are in the middle of the process of sorting out the meanings of everything; trying to find what it looks like, what it sounds like, what it feels like. If you are not in this state then you are not learning. It is the phase the psychologists call "cognitive". It is the planning and strategy-making stage. It is the stage when you are making all the important linkages between one element of the subject and another. I am not sure if it is possible to skip this stage, but even if you could it would be the worst possible thing you could do because this is a fundamental.

Sport psychology identifies **three** stages. Learn them and you can put disappointment behind you.

The **Cognitive** – thinking about it, trying to understand it, making sense of it, even finding out how to know when you have grasped it.

The **Associative** (Practice phase) – in physical activities such as skiing, once you understand it, you need to start practising it, and that is the associative phase. You'll know when you have entered this phase, because whatever it is you are trying to do, it will happen at first just once. That is the moment; that brilliant moment when you first know that this is something that truly is going to be within your compass because you just DID IT! What Franz Klammer used to call the "Aha!" moment. As soon as it happens once, you know you are capable of it. This is something you are going to be able to do. You have changed your belief! Few feelings are better. All you need now is to do the repeats, pay your dues, and not succumb to temporary setbacks. From one time in a hundred, you will gradually increase the number of successful attempts until one day, one glorious day, you can make it happen every time. As Frank Dick said – **Persist.**

The **Autonomous** -when that day dawns, the day will not be far off when you find yourself thinking back over some occasion, and finding that it happened every time and you were not even thinking about it! When that day dawns you will be in the autonomous phase and not only will you know about it, but more importantly you will *know* it!

Then you move on to the next task or development and the process re-iterates, again and again.

Apply this to your skiing and increase your enjoyment

I said this book isn't a theoretical one and I meant it. Here's how you can put your understanding of this three-phase process to real practical use in helping you not only to ski better, but to stop beating yourself up every time some attempt at something does not go the way you expected or intended.

Next time you try something, and what you get is something different to what you were hoping for, you can put it in the context of Cognitive, Associative or Autonomic. (Thinking; Practicing; or Automatic). Which phase does it indicate you are currently in? This could equally apply to something as apparently mundane as repairing some device or other, or making out the perfect shopping list.

If you find yourself cursing yourself for being a "fool" or being "useless" – "Oh … will I ever get this"? – you can instead put it into a framework that will help you, instead of hindering you. You can say – "Hey, what do I expect; all this means is that I'm in the Associative or practice phase, I should *expect* that sometimes it will work and as yet oftentimes it won't. That's o.k. I'm making progress, and making progress is more fun than arriving." If you do this, you will be happier, and your learning will accelerate.

If you find you just cannot "get a handle on it", or you can't "see where this is coming from", or it just doesn't "ring any bells" for you, then all that is telling you, is that you are as yet in the cognitive phase; not yet reached the 'practice' stage. You are still thinking it through. Well, that's fine. What is wrong with that? If that is the phase you are in, with respect to that bit of the activity, then that just **is**. It says nothing whatever about you, nothing about your potential, how you "ought" to be; what you "should" be doing; or any of that self-denigration. There is no value to be assigned to it. It just is.

Above all else take this to heart – the perhaps lower outcome you are currently getting (compared to what you hoped for) is not a predictor of what you are capable of achieving in the future. Ever.

Furthermore, if you spend your skiing time not acknowledging at what stage of learning you currently are, your only possible reference point can be the ultimate target, – expert all-terrain skiing. The goal that is farthest away. The one that will take the longest time to get to. The most uncertain. The one shrouded in the mountain mists of the distant future. How is that for a recipe for success? Relate only to this distant dream (and we need to dream, but cleverly) and you will always be falling short, and that will be damaging to you. You don't have to buy-in to that destructive model.

Don't beat yourself up.

I spent years giving myself endless "internal g.b.h." because of this. All I could see before me was that much desired but far off dream. The distance between where I was and where I wanted ultimately to get to was enormous, so everything I did was a disappointment; no matter that it was an improvement on what had gone before; no matter that I was getting better. Believe me, you do not want to put yourself through the suffering I did, and you certainly do not have to.

What a hopeless way to go through life. What a destructive process to build into our attempts to become an expert skier, or anything else. All it did was make me impatient, and "*anticipation keeps you waiting*" (A Carly Simon lyric). All it did was to frustrate me.

I now think that it was a form of conceit, or at least a lack of humility.

Looking back on it, what right did I have to think that I should be anywhere on the learning curve other than where I was?

The question that it would have been more instructive to ask, would have been – "Why should I **not** be at this point on the learning curve?" I was where I was, because of the things I had done, the quality of my teachers, how long I had skied, and the decisions I had made in the past with respect to skiing. Where I was, on the learning curve, was simply appropriate. Indeed it can't be anything else, no matter where you are.

I guess it is natural to be a bit disappointed when you first come to know enough to become aware that you are in the Conscious Incompetence phase – after all in my case up until then I really thought I was a pretty good skier, so no wonder I got pulled up a bit short, because I wasn't. But once I came to understand that learning is not about "content" but is about "process", the whole world changed for me. For the better and it can for you too.

So take a step back. Look at your skiing in a proper context. You may have been skiing for twenty years, but for how many minutes of that time, have you actually been focused, with expert help, on one small precise movement, or outcome, or understanding? Probably not many. How often has any teacher or instructor, one-on-one with you, been helping you to really *understand* what is happening? Probably fewer.

It's no one's "fault" that your skiing is currently at its present level; it is simply a fact. No matter where our skiing is, that is precisely where it is appropriate for it to be. This is a fact which does not carry with it any implications about your intellect, your physical abilities, your worth as a human being, and certainly nothing about your potential! And you do have potential. The really good news is that **you can make big improvements from here** There is absolutely no doubt about it.

THE M.A.S.T.E.R. PRINCIPLE

This easy-to-remember mnemonic was created by a Learning Trainer called Jayne Nicholl, who wrote the book Open Sesame. Ms Nicholl works in the subject of Accelerated Learning, a subject which over the last fifteen or so years, has opened up huge learning potentials all over the world, although regrettably it has had little impact in the UK.

We live in a time of fantastically rapid change; a time when you cannot rely on much that you already know being of any use in a few years' time. Clearly then, this is a time when the ability to learn efficiently is a premium resource. The M.A.S.T.E.R mnemonic reminds us of the steps you can employ if you want to learn anything and in our present case, how to ski a lot better.

I will not be going deeply into the subject of Accelerated Learning, I'm not an expert; I will skim over its more arcane points, but we can use it as an extra tool to get practical results in your skiing.

I have adapted the letters M.A.S.T.E.R to stand for just slightly different constructs to Nicholl's mnemonic:

It goes like this : –

Motivate your Mind.

Assemble **A**ll the information you can find on the subject; don't second guess whether it is "good" or "bad" at this stage.

Sort the information and **Search** for its meaning.

Test yourself for what you know.

Experiment!! , and

Review, often.

This set of six letters has power to help you MASTER your ability to learn, not only how to change your skiing, but to learn anything. Follow this sequence (which will continue to re-iterate as you proceed), and you can not only accelerate your learning, you can avoid a lot of stress, disappointment and self-denigration.

I will introduce you to Techniques, Tools and Tactics, as we progress, to help you incorporate this process into your own skiing in practical ways.

8.

Chapter 8: Change, not easy but simple.

Change. There is just one rule, and just two options.

"Change? Change? Who wants change; things are bad enough already!" (Lord Salisbury to Queen Victoria.)

"I guess you only change, when the pain of changing gets to be less than the pain of staying as you are". (Anonymous heroin addict; W. Virginia. USA)

Change is simple. Being willing to change isn't. "How many psychologists does it take to change a light bulb? Only one, but the light bulb must be ready to change". People even find giving up smoking is easy – once they are ready to do it.

Simple, and yet often the hardest thing in the world to do is change. Why is this?

I have worked with individuals, teams, and corporations. Everybody says they want to bring about change, but few ever do it.

I once spent a year, trying to help a company change its processes, at their request, because the then current ones were leading to steady decline. Every single board member nodded sagely when asked "Do you want to bring about beneficial changes in the company's behaviour?" The MD was pleased that they nodded. He would have been more pleased if they had changed!

Nothing happened of course. Six months after the start of the project no changes were evident, and profits continued to fall. It was frustrating. Finally, I requested a special board meeting, and at that meeting I first of all asked the same question again and got the same reassuring replies. Then I asked if it would be alright if I said exactly the same thing, but in a more abbreviated and straight-forward form; a less "management speak" form. Permission was granted. I then said – "As from tomorrow at 9 a.m. things are going to be done differently around here, at your desk and everyone else's!" The consternation on the assembled faces was a sight to see.

The company did not change, instead it chose to fail, and went bust a year later.

"When you come to a fork in the road, take it." (Yogi Berra)

I now believe that if folk don't change, it is because they don't want to. When you want to, it's simple. I didn't say it is easy; I said it's simple. If you really do want change, then there is just one simple rule, leading to two simple options.

Key "take-aways".

The rule.

If you want changed outcomes – **do something else***. When you have decided that you are prepared to do something else, you have only two simple options open to you –*

The options

Option 1 : Do something ***different.***
Option 2 : Do something ***differently.***

There are **no other possibilities**. Isn't that marvelous? Life is so simple. Let us take a skiing example. Suppose you believe that in order to "do a turn" (I hate this phrase), you need to "turn your skis" (I hate this one as well – I'll tell you why later). However, your 'turns' are not very effective. You are not sure before they happen, what they are going to be like. When they happen they seem almost to come from nowhere.

Many of my pupils have told me that they never quite knew either why or how their skis got them down the slope in once piece at all ! The whole process was too problematical and unpredictable to deliver any confidence – especially any confidence that it would happen satisfactorily next time, and the time after that. Small wonder people begin to lose confidence. Finally, you may find you can only make one kind of 'turn' with one kind of radius, because you only have the one way of doing it, and it works well sometimes in some circumstances, but not in all the others.

When I first became an instructor I had an adult pupil on the dry slope who perfectly illustrated this. He did exactly the same thing all evening long, looking quite proficient (which is what he wanted, i.e. to *look* proficient). Never did anything different: his wife thought he was an expert. Every year he came back from the Alps with an injury, because he only had one spanner in his bag and inevitably came across a nut it didn't fit. His wife and I got her to be much better than him.

So let us imagine that changing your skiing sufficiently has not proved possible for you as yet. But now we have a change *process*. So remember Rule 1? Do something else. Something other than what? Before you can do something else you first need to become aware of what you are currently doing. Until then, even if you did something else, you may not be able to recognise that you did.

So, first find out what you are doing.

To take an instance, maybe what you are doing is 'turning the ski', because your belief is that this is the way to "do a turn". OK, now we can move on to the two options.

Option 1 – we could do something *other* than 'turn the ski' – i.e. Don't turn the ski, but do something else, and see what happens. Or ..
Option 2 – we could 'turn the ski' differently and find out what we get.

How might we do that? We could pivot it – Ealier· Later· More· Less· Quicker· Slower, hold it longer. More forcefully· More gently · More suddenly· More progressively

You can now make a choice between options 1 & 2, and then take action. Find a gentle slope. I stress a gentle slope, with a long run-out, so you will feel safe. DO the new action. **Only** the new selected action. Don't change more than that one thing. Keep it simple. Then, be aware of any difference in outcome you achieve.

You will notice that I did not suggest you did something "better". I did not suggest trying harder. Just do something different or do something differently. You will get a different outcome, and so long as you notice what the change is, you are on the way to becoming a better skier, or a better anything for that matter.

This is the happiest experiment you can make because it cannot fail you. No matter what happens, you are in profit. If an improvement occurs, it tells you something and hints at the way ahead. If matters get worse, it tells you something and hints at the way ahead. Voila! Every one a winner. Do not change two things at once. Only pick one of the items in the list of pivoting actions above for example, and work with that one for a while, always checking in what ways the outcome changes. (Think back to my first time on the firing range – you need feedback). And so you don't scare yourself, make sure you picked a really easy slope.

You will notice which changes work better, and which changes don't. You won't need to spend ages deciding with which ones to continue. Do remember though, that while you will be developing new techniques, you will not become skillful with them until you have repeated them many times. So don't expect this process to "magic" you into better skiing; you still need to 'pay your dues' as our transatlantic cousins put it. What this *will* do is get you into the "practice" phase. That is to say, it will work now-and-again at first, then increasingly often.

Be warned however; change may well *feel* worse at first, even if the outcome is an improvement. This is because the habituated behaviours you already have, are comfortable – you are used to them; this is why we stick with them and why they are resistant to change. Be especially careful not to equate a feeling of discomfort or "newness" with a *worsening* of performance. Your new way of doing things is bound to feel strange at first – another reason folk resist change.

Investigate the **feelings** so you can identify precisely what you are doing. Investigate the **outcomes** to identify what you get in exchange for those changed things you are doing. When all you are doing is what you have done before but slightly differently, that's not drastic change is it? Not very scary.

To prove this to yourself, try playing this little game, right now, as you sit reading this.

Take a moment, be calm, and then clasp your hands with your fingers "interleaving". Give it few repeats, unclasp them and clasp them again. Then take a note of which index finger (your left or your right) is always the one on top.

Then whichever it is, unclasp your hands and clasp them again but this time deliberately with the *other* index finger on top. I'll take a bet that it feels quite awkward, and yet it is just as effective. That is our psychologist friends' "habituated behaviours" for you. Simple, isn't it?

"Simple, is best". *(Gerald Harrison, Coach)*

9.

Chapter 9: Just Three Essentials

Three essentials only.

Frank Dick, once one of Britain's most senior Olympic athletics coaches was always of the opinion that in order to achieve some goal, you need to have three elements in place; but they must all be in place, miss one and you will miss out. He said those three elements are:

1. You must want whatever it is. (Perhaps quite a lot)
2. You must truly believe it is possible for you. (With enough application and time why should it not be?)
3. You will need to persist. (In the face of inevitable set-backs).

Mildly wanting it may not be enough. You may need to want it passionately. You may need to be prepared to pay a high cost for it, to make sacrifices, to "work" at it, if you can describe skiing as work. If you want to win a gold medal at the Olympics you will need to be so committed to the goal that persisting will be relatively easy; you will be prepared to train hard when you least feel like it; even give up drink! Perhaps we'll give the Olympics a miss!

You will see that in order to have all these three elements in place and working for you, it is not your feet, or your legs, or your ski poles you need – it is your mind; and your mind needs to be under your control.

The good news is that if you really do want to be an in- control and skillful skier, you *can* be, because even if you don't yet believe it's possible, you can change your beliefs (I'll be showing you how). You can find many ways to help you in your desire to persist, and many ways to overcome the forces that want to stop you.

If at this point you are quietly groaning to yourself that in your case this won't apply and you are doomed, then stop that right now. Let me tell you a little story about a late-starting middle-aged skier who was stuck "on the plateau."

This skier was unwittingly being held back by an underlying unconsciously held belief. The belief was that – "we are what we are"; that change is a virtual impossibility; that you are born a certain way, thinking in a certain way, acting in a certain way and getting what you get because it is inevitable. *"I can't change. This is the way I am, and I wish it were not, but there it is, there's nothing I can do. I'm never likely to really get any good."* This is how this skier thought, and it came from his belief system. It was a system that had received considerable reinforcement from others who wanted to stop him in his tracks.

By accident this skier came across some psychological concepts that were quite intriguing; concepts which promised big returns if he employed them. To his credit, he put his cynicism away in a safe place for a while (didn't throw it away, you never know when it might be needed!) and gave these ideas a fair crack of the whip. He committed to actually **using** them. (We get good at what we do, remember?). In time it worked.

He made a clear list of what he wanted, what his goals were, and he wrote them down. He wrote them down as a "story" that depicted these goals having already happened. The psychologists have proved that writing things down has a seminal effect on our psyche. He kept reviewing what he had written, and slowly came to believe it was possible. That made it easier to keep at it when the going got tough, when disappointments came along, and when others tried to stop him achieving his goal.

He even committed to paying the not inconsiderable psychological price of standing in front of a mirror, and saying to his reflected image, things like *"I ski centred and balanced"*, when in fact at the time he knew he didn't. He felt foolish. But after only a few weeks, it worked.

The "story" was a little 'dream' in which his wife was sitting on the deck of the mountain restaurant at the foot of the black run that he dreamed of skiing, sipping wine and waiting for him to join her in the sunshine after he had skied it. He imagined what it felt like, proudly pointing out where he had just come down, looking back at what he'd done.

It happened exactly as he had written it. His skiing wasn't much good, but his motivation had made achieving his goal possible. That skier went from ropey intermediate to International Coach in under six years. That skier was me of course, and I'm no superman. If I can do it, you can do it. You have the same brain I have; you have the same body I have, (pity, I know) and the same opportunity I had. You may well be younger than I was.

You can have the mental control you want; here are a few considerations –

Here's a very worthwhile exercise to do.

Decide **with precision** what you want in the long term. Write it down. This is your "dream" goal; perhaps a long way off.
Decide very precisely what you want **right now or next** (whenever "now" is; could be on this stretch of ski slope, right now, for example, or could be next week, next ski hol ….)
Date it. Without a date a goal is not a goal it is only a dream.
Develop your motivation (the story above was one way)
Develop mental strength (We'll look at ways to do this too, with help from Sport Psychologists). It's not Voodoo.

I read of a perfect example of changing a limiting belief. It shows clearly that WE control our own beliefs; they are not delivered by some external agency.

One of Britain's up and coming swimmers, achieved a minor placing – 12th or something – in the Olympics. He wanted to win the gold medal in the next Olympics just four years away. He and his coach estimated that the winning time would be faster than this year's, off which he was already some distance anyway. They calculated the required improvement as about 4 seconds, which in his swimming event was huge.

At first this was daunting and stood a good chance of destroying his motivation because the possibility of it seemed unbelievable to him. His belief was negative. He couldn't believe that this could be something of which he might be capable.

Then he began to use his mind on it. He worked out how many training sessions he was prepared to put in every week. He multiplied that by 208 (every week for four years). He calculated what that translated into if he divided 4 seconds by the number of training sessions, or the number of lengths, or the time spent training.

It worked out at an average of a fraction of a second improvement per session. He then discovered that this fraction was somewhat shorter than a typical eye-blink. He began to feel that he might well have this rate of improvement within him, if he trained hard and stuck to his guns. His goal had now become not "4 seconds off my time". It had become 0.00 something quicker by the end of the next training session. On average.

He did not expect it to be easy, and smooth going. He expected it to be hard work, and to need resolute application. He expected set-backs. Most of all he expected correctly that improvement would not be one smooth upward curve – sometimes it would go well and for periods it wouldn't. But he had changed his belief about himself – this was something that it seemed reasonable to believe to be possible. For him. He now had hope.

He won the Gold Medal in the next Olympics. This is a true story. (But I can't remember his name!)

Successes, however small, breed successes.
John Shedden. Senior Coach

This is different from “Success breeds Success”. It suggests a **process.** However small, each success provides a foundation for another. That is why skillful goal setting is not the same as merely setting big targets.

It is the placing ahead of you, of a series of anticipated stepping stones. Landing on each one gives you the take-off point to reach for the next one. It also means that if after trying a few times you find you cannot reach that next one – get another stone and place it inbetween, so you can. There is no point in falling in the river, that won’t get you anywhere, except drowned.

10.

Chapter 10: Imagery. Imagination and Rituals

The incredible power of your imagination

This is an important chapter. This chapter has plenty of things in it that you will really benefit from not only reading and understanding, but actually doing! Practise them. It will pay you handsomely. It will cost you nothing. You will need neither a slope, nor snow. Any quiet moments anywhere will be perfect – a nice warm bath is good.

The chapter is mostly about "imagery". Imagery is such a powerful technique that I felt it worthwhile really going over it in some detail. If there is much in here that is confusing, and after a few "goes" at it, you are still in a fog, then do feel free to email me at **bobski@bobski.com** I'll gladly help.

There are many "mind games" that work – Meditation; Relaxation; Imagery; Concentration; Self-Motivation. All top performers in sport use them and work at getting skilful with them. It's a pity our schools, universities and businesses don't do the same. The effect on the country could be miraculous. The most recent and excellent example is our top woman tennis player Johanna Konta for whom it has transformed her life not just her tennis.

Of all of them, "Imagery" is perhaps the most powerful. The effective use of imagery (imagining) has profound effects on learning and performance, unique from other mental and physical processes.

A key "take-away".

*The primary purpose of developing skill in the use of imagery is to develop the ability to **retain, recall and re-play** the key perceptual-motor elements of performance. When you can do this, you will then be able not only to recall in vivid detail what your performance was "like", but also be able to **project into the future,** images of the elements of ideal performance.*

This is not something beyond your capabilities; Ms. Konta is not a different kind of being to us, she just came across these things and realised their value.

You can then use the images as goals, as well as guiding principles and calibration pointers. The process of using imagery means that everything you imagine is directly within your control. You deliberately choose to eliminate incomplete, inappropriate, negative or ill-timed images that can have very negative effects, and are to be avoided. So the *process* matters.

"Imagery" is not some new technique. Neither is it mystical. It always has existed and it is used by all of us some of the time, though often not consciously. It serves memory, learning, creating, planning, and performance. Anyone planning tonight's meal "sees" it in his mind's eye: anyone planning the next bit of joinery woodwork does the same. But this does not mean that we are automatically good at it; we need to practice it.

Imagery appears to be integrally linked to perception and action. For that reason it has powerful potential for evoking understanding and bringing about change. It is highly effective when used for specific purposes. You can use imagery to bring about desired mental states, learning and performance.

Skiing is technical and physical so there is a huge amount of information to be dealt with in the execution of a skiing run. Question: How do *you* handle all these technical aspects? Do you find that if you try to "talk" your way through a run, all that happens is confusion? In a physical activity like skiing, it is not possible to use words to control your actions *while you are skiing*. Partly this is because there isn't time, and more importantly it is because words are merely descriptions. They are less than that, they are just labels for things.

Language is a representational system that is good for some things but not for controlling your performance *as you perform*. Good for planning what you will do, but less good as you are doing it. Fortunately we have other representational systems and imagery is one of them.

Imagery is not just a visual system. What we mean in psychology by imagery is the wordless imagining of the information we have stored (or can imagine!) by using any of our representational systems :

These systems are – Seeing, Feeling, Hearing, Smelling, Tasting, and Proprioception.

Join me in this next little game, it is quite instructive. First, a "sound" one. Do you have a mobile phone?

hink – What does it sound like when it rings?

When you read that question, you didn't *describe it*, you just "heard" it? Imagined it.

Now here's a "visual" one.

Close your eyes and think – When you open your front door, – what's the first thing that you see?

And when you read this question, did you have to say "table", or "carpet" or whatever it happened to be, before you could "see" it, or did you "see" it first, and then maybe scrabble for a word to describe it?

In skiing or other physical activities it is our kinaesthetic imagining which is of greatest importance. In other words what you *feel* – the way you feel all the movements in motion and their outcomes. Unfortunately not many of us initially are any good at it. Not many of us are naturals. Young children are great at it, but we lose the ability as we begin to process our incoming data more and more by using words.

And perceptive readers will have noticed that in the two little exercises above I chose to use different "representational systems" – Hearing, and Sight.

Here's a quick try-out:

- Sit somewhere safe, close your eyes and relax.
- Imagine yourself on a gentle sunlit freshly pisted wide slope with no one about except you. You can let the sun be shining if you like. Imagine that you are about to conduct a "feeling" experiment in total safety.
- Your goal is simply to get to know if you can actually feel the underside of your feet as you ski. Nothing else. "Stand" there (eyes closed) for a few moments in a narrow snow plough and determine that you will hold that plough for the next 200 metres of imaginary skiing (you're not trying to "ski", you're trying to feel).
- As you are "standing" there, imagine yourself being aware of the pressures on the soles of your feet. Where are the pressures? Are they the same on both? What happens if you just slightly lift one, but not quite off the ground?
- Imagine setting off, slowly and gently, and skiing a small series of slow linked arcs in your snow plough. When do you feel the most pressure? Notice how it's always on the outer foot of the arc until you have finished with that arc and begin changing to the next one. When is the pressure equal? When does it begin to change (it's as you change direction). Feel how one foot has most pressure and the other almost none if you ski a little faster in the arcs.
- When you feel it, is it on the inside edge of your foot, or the outside? Is it on your toes or your heel?

- When you have "skied" a little way, gently stop, and "see" yourself standing safely at the piste's edge, being really pleased you have enhanced your sense of feeling as you ski.

Believe me, this activity really does work. And it is so accessible; you can do it any time. you don't have to wait until you are on the slopes.

Using language is a form of serial processing, and that's just too slow for this purpose. What we need as we are trying to improve our physical performance is a method of parallel processing, and nature provided us with it. What we need to do is get back to using it both more, and more effectively, like we did when we were kids.

Not only that, but when you "image" you can do it in real time. You can capture (and even predict) the dynamic flow of the movements, or the pictures, or the sounds. Imagining is very like the actual performance. Indeed **the same neural pathways are "fired" when you *imagine* something as are fired when you *do* it.** There is no mental difference, and that is why it is so powerful.

Images (using all our senses not just sight) are rich in information – they are the closest memories and representations of our perception and our experience.

You can use your imaging powers (your powers of imagination) to recall past experience, or to predict experiences, and to live right now experiences you will have in the future. That's almost doing MAGIC! and we all have that power within our power.

Here's another one, from the "future".

You can conjure up an image of something that has not yet happened, but that you are looking back upon from an imaginary future even further ahead than when it "happened". Is that not amazing?

I did it, you'll recall, in my 'story' in the previous chapter about meeting my wife after my (as yet not done) ski run. If you have a conscious advance "image" of the ideal of some aspect of your performance, this gives your unconscious mind a datum line against which to judge in real time, that aspect of your performance. You may not have time to consciously and in real time adjust your performance against the ideal, but you won't need to, your unconscious mind will be able to do it for you.

This is particularly useful if you have "bad" habits. If you have some performance technicalities which you automatically do, but which you know are inappropriate or dysfunctional but hard to shed, you can enhance your "unlearning" of these, and further facilitate the learning of modified or replacement behaviours through the use of imagery.

To improve your skiing, what are the images that are going to be important to you? Which of your senses are of importance? (Not just sight, that's for sure! But probably not smell or taste.)

You will want to become more aware of the information you receive through the relevant representational systems. In skiing that will be feeling, seeing, and possibly hearing. Taste and smell don't matter much, but proprioception will be vital.

Proprioception is the "sixth sense" that enables you to touch your nose with your finger with your eyes shut. It helps us know internally, where all our "bits" are.

You'll also benefit from developing an ability to become more aware of what you feel – for example what feelings you get on the soles of your feet; what feelings you get in your ankles, or what you feel against your shins. Or becoming aware of tension across your shoulders for example.

You will need to practice to become more expert at noticing what you are feeling and perhaps linking those feelings as you have them, to other sensory inputs such as what you see or what you hear. There is a number of papers on my website at bobski.com. referring to this business of how to "knowtice" – a word I made up combining knowing with noticing.

It is not an easy technique with which to become skillful, so how might you actually go about it when on the slopes? You may not be able to rapidly get good at being continuously aware, so the best way to start is just to remind yourself now and again (a few times) each run, to check on what you feel, or see, or hear, (not together, one at a time) and see if you can remember those once you've stopped.

This is yet another reason why, if you are consciously training, it is hopeless to do complete runs top to bottom – you need to do the run in a series of short sections. If you don't your learning rate will fall faster than an avalanche.

Ask yourself – what is the feeling when something goes well? Careful here! It is not **how** you are feeling, it is **what** you are feeling. **What** is the feeling in your feet right now, in your boots as you stand there? What is the feeling in your arms as your skis make an arc? And so on. Standing at the edge of the piste, don't be unwilling to play the relaxed eyes-closed game you tried above, and in that way recall the most recent bit of your ski run.

It is important, very important, that you do not make ANY judgements of the quality of technique you are employing while you are working toward developing this higher level awareness. It is quite likely in the early stages that while you are doing this your skiing technique on those runs will actually worsen. Too much to think about. Your skiing technique while playing this game doesn't matter, and you should "let it go". The reason for this is that while you are focusing on this task, **your goal is to become aware of becoming aware.** Your goal is not to ski at your best, or even to ski in any particular way at all. Therefore your attention is being focused on your **awareness** of sensory input. Not the outputs.

You will not have sufficient attentional span or focus to allow yourself to attend to issues of skiing technique while trying this out (that can come later, perhaps – perhaps not). It would be wrong to make any judgement about your technique at this stage. Just concentrate on finding out how aware of your senses you can be. One sense at a time only.

The following is the first phase of developing your imagery ability. In this stage your goal is to begin to develop the ability to notice and recall your sensory inputs; what you can become aware of seeing, feeling or hearing.

Here are some pointers to using imagery to improve your technique.

Treat these as learning objectives.

Ask yourself what sensory images you can usually retain after a short ski run.

Can you re-play the "video tape", the "audio tape", or the "feelio" tape of what happened?·

If so but only partially, at what point(s) does your ability to do this start and finish?

If not at all, that's quite normal, and it is an important learning.

One of the "blocks" to developing this powerful ability is trying too hard to get too many things right at once.· We will choose a simple task, in a non-challenging environment. This is important. You will not develop this ability on slopes which are steep for you, or in bad snow conditions, or other challenging environments.

The first goal is for you to be able after completion of the task, to "notice what you noticed": to be aware of what you noticed. This is not easy. But it is worthwhile.

The task is not to perform in any particular way. At this juncture just do it, and how it happens is how it happens. Just explore what you notice, or what you don't notice. The game is "awareness". So it is not a game you can lose.

If you have great difficulty with this you will not be alone, many do in the early stages of their development of this ability. When you are having difficulty, set yourself a simpler task and simpler goal on an even easier slope.

Set yourself the goal to begin with of noticing just one of your perceptual representational systems – choose either to notice what you feel, or what you see, or what you hear. For the time being ignore all your senses except the targeted one. IF at the end of the run you find that you noticed something with any of the other senses, treat that as a mighty bonus!

After considerable practice at this, you may become quite skilful at it. Certainly that is the goal. However it is only half the story. You may become very good indeed at recalling your perceptions in any of your representational systems, yet at the same time be fooling yourself!

It is common for us at this stage to begin to believe our perceptions; but they can easily be wrong. They may well be vivid and lifelike, but therein lies the rub, life-*like,* not actual.

It is all too easy for us to now be imagining that something is happening, when in fact it is not. So now we need to be able to check our perceptions against some more objective reality. What really matters is for you to know through your new and developing internal awareness system, which sights / sounds / feelings actually correlate with the quality of performance you want to get from correct execution of some particular movements in motion. Now is the time to focus on being aware of the outcomes.

HERE ARE SOME MORE POINTERS

To do these comparisons you need an expert external observer, and possibly the use of video.

To make sense of the post-execution discussions it is essential that you have jointly agreed on the task, and on the one element upon which your attention will be focused.

You may then interrogate your perceptions through the use of your newly-burgeoning imagery ability, and your coach can then discuss with you what he/she saw.

In time the very best feedback is what you can recall, through your use of real-time awareness and your imaging ability. The coach's feedback will be as accurate as he or she can make it, but you should remember that they are just an eye witness, and eye witness accounts are always subject to distortion and mis-perception. This is true even though your coach will have worked at least as hard as you on developing their present-moment awareness and their ability to use imaging to enhance their recall of what they perceived as you performed the task.

This also gives a partial clue as to why watching an expert skier, if you are not a trained and expert watcher, is not a good way to attempt to learn.

A Neuro-linguistic (NLP) Technique.

Because well-formed images in any of the sensory representational systems (fancy term for your senses) are such a rich source of information storage, and similarly seem to have the ability to connect this information with our feelings, thoughts and emotions. NLP has developed a technique for linking these with what is referred to in the discipline as "anchors".

Imagery can very powerfully assist us to generate at will any desired mental state. Using imagery can enable us to project forward to an anticipated event, a desirable mental state, and a required behaviour pattern.

The technique needs to be learnt and practised, just as a physical technique does, and follows a series of simple, powerful, steps.

Here's an example you can practice (at any time).

- First, get into a relaxed state using your preferred relaxation technique.
- Next, recall an occasion in the past when you either had the now-desired mental state, or performed particularly satisfactorily, or both.
- The objective now, is to connect these experiences with a visual, and auditory, and physical cue.
- While recalling the past experience, you can "play" with the image to enhance it: you could make the picture bigger, or you could brighten the colours. You could remember what you were hearing at the time and make it louder. You can enjoy those feelings again, and immerse yourself in them.enhance it: you could make the picture bigger, or you could brighten the colours. You could remember what you were hearing at the time and make it louder. You can enjoy those feelings again, and immerse yourself in them.
- When the imaged experience is at its peak for you, then,
- Say a chosen "cue" word to yourself.
- See a suitable picture or simple image.
- Make some kind of simple physical movement – something you would not normally do in other circumstances. For example, let's say you are preparing for you next chance to practice skiing something really steep; something that might otherwise "freak you out".
- Bring up the memory of the last time you surprised yourself with a pleasing performance on something steeper than you normally ski.
- Just as it peaks, you could say (or even shout out loud) "Control!"

- You could "picture" the edge of your ski's tip digging into the slope as you came round the arc, and
- You could knock together your two fists as if knocking the top of your ski pole handles together.
- As soon as you do that "knocking" imagine yourself immediately setting off.

Practise this in your imagination before you go skiing, and when the time comes you will find it easy to go through this preparation, and it will stand you in good stead. It will get you mentally prepared, and with the right mind-set you can do anything!

Let me refer you to Johanna Konta again, or indeed any top tennis player. Recall what they do prior to serving. They will have a ritual of behaviour; Rafa Nadal is a classic example. The things they do **never** change; they are exactly the same every time. Why? Because that takes their mind into a well-practiced comfort zone, and sequesters all those influences that could distract them. Not the least of these is a fear of not succeeding. And at the end of their ritual there will be one final thing that they do (Johanna always bounces the ball four times on the first service, but only three times on the second). This final thing – such as knocking your ski pole grips together – must **immediately** be followed by action. No delay. Because it is this which tells your subconscious that preparation is finished, that you are prepared to accept the challenge, and that **now** is the time.

Some key aspects of this powerful technique are:

Key "take-aways".

1. Work hard not to allow yourself to feel embarrassed or 'silly' doing these things
2. Relax yourself
3. Build up your image to a peak
4. Choose three cues – visual, auditory, and kinaesthetic.

It works.

What you are working on is the changing of your beliefs. When we are very young our beliefs about ourselves are very much imposed by external influences – get told that you are a naughty boy (accompanied by wagging fingers and angry expressions) and voila! that's how you think of yourself. From then on you will feel some cognitive dissonance if your behaviours *don't* map onto that framework. So increasingly you feel comfortable playing the role of naughty boy. And uncomfortable not doing, or being told we are "good" occasionally.

But we don't have to carry on like that now we are grown up. Beliefs are not immutable; we can change them. They are our beliefs; we can do with them whatever we like. We created them, we can destroy them. It is entirely legitimate.

If one of your current beliefs is that you cannot, or at least are unlikely to be able, to improve your skiing, then you can choose to keep that belief. Or not. You could choose another belief. You could choose to believe that you are as good as anyone else, and that there is no reason at all for believing that you could not become a much better skier, provided you find a way of going about it right.

That, by the way, objectively, is the truth.

Believing in yourself takes work!

Beliefs are changed enactively, by doing things. Cognitively, by thinking things. Vicariously, by imagining or watching things. And emotively by addressing your reactions to circumstances.

You can overcome –

- Anxiety, by employing proven, simple mental techniques
- Self-doubt, similarly, such as positive self-talk
- Pain – mental or physical – by re-labelling it
- Brooding, by using mental techniques such as affirmations and achievement reminders.
- A sense of 'losing' or 'failing' by getting to know how to set effective goals.

These are just techniques and they can be learnt. Olympians use them all the time. Change doesn't happen – you need to make it happen.
Build yourself a "ritual".I strongly recommend you to develop one for yourself. It does not have to be anything wildly obvious, but it needs to be routine. Do it every time. Something thoughtful; something tactile; something visual; some movement. Anything. And build-in one final thing you do.

So what will you get out of doing this? What will it do for you?

● Firstly these rituals set the stage for maximizing your self-efficacy expectations.

● Secondly, they comprehensively minimize the opportunity for you to stand there rehearsing self-defeating thoughts.

● Thirdly, they keep you grounded and help set you up for productive effort.

● You can utilise your ritual, if it pleases you, specifically to incorporate recollections of past success. They have been shown to help initiate problem-solving modes of thinking.

• Your ritual will help make your environment more familiar, feel safer, and help you to be more comfortable. But it won't do it by itself – you have to do it.

One final word of caution – when you succeed, remember it's **you** who succeeded, not your ritual. **You**.

A note of caution: if you experience serious anxiety or fear before, or even during a ski run, do not expect to be able to fully conquer it using *only* mental techniques. You cannot *trick* your mind into confidence. Confidence needs to be based on some objective reality, and in our case that means having sufficient technical skill to do what needs doing. The two go together. Together they *will* take you further on your journey to skillful skiing. Neither one is a substitute for the other.

11.

Chapter 11: What's a "well-formed outcome"? How it helps you.

How to develop a pre-formed "Well-formed-Outcome".

In chapter "Just three things needed", about the "1-2-3 Steps to getting what you want", the first requisite step was to want it.

But the alert reader will have noticed that there is one tacit step before that. You have to choose what "it" is going to be; and in order to become really motivated by the idea, you will need to use perhaps the most powerful weapon in your mental armoury – your imagination.

In Neuro Linguistic Programming the creation of this idea is known as generating your desired "well-formed outcome". A vague, diaphanous idea will be of little use, but a precise one, which you can feel, see, hear and perhaps smell will be a tool of great power which will, at the level of your subconscious, be constantly and quietly directing all you think and do, toward the achievement of your goal. Nowadays they call it "nudging" but it has been around a long time.

I referred above to my own case when I created my own "story", wrote it down, and "lived" it over and over again long before I got to the slopes. What I did was pure N.L.P. My goal for that season – it was only about my third ever week – was "ski a black run". It seems a silly goal to me now, and took no account of how *well* I was to ski it, but at least I had a clear goal.

What I did was to hand-write a story with me as the central character (it was only half a page long), and in it I saw myself finishing the (imaginary) run, skiing across to my wife who was on a veranda sipping a glass of wine in the sunshine, and then looking up the mountain with her, and showing her what I had done.

It is important to hand-write it; I don't know why, but writing things down dramatically alters how they go into your subconscious. I could **picture** myself with her. I could **hear** myself telling her how challenging and exciting it had been. I could **feel** the tiredness in my legs and glow of satisfaction and pride in my achievement. And as I have just this moment realised, I can still "remember" it vividly.

Did it work? I can't guarantee that is what did it, but I did do my first black run that holiday, and I did show it to my wife, and I did re-live it with her; she was even on the deck of a mountain restaurant! I have used this technique many times since, in many different circumstances. I am utterly convinced of it, as indeed I now know, are thousands of world class and Olympian athletes.

There are certain rules for creating your well-formed outcome, and certain ways to use it, and I applied them to my story. Firstly, your well-formed outcome must be *positive*. Planning to not do something, or to avoid something won't work. This is one of the reasons that so many folk find giving up snacking so difficult; they only focus on giving up, instead of the positives of getting more done, looking slimmer, feeling fitter, saving money and so on. It's no good imagining a story whose basis is "I'm going to not feel afraid"; you need one that says something more like – "I'm skiing this new challenge like I've never skied before, and feeling absolutely exhilarated."

Next, your outcome must be something which you control, not something in the control of others, or merely random. In the case I've mentioned the outcome depended on me; only I could bring it about. If I didn't, nobody else could.

Then you have to decide, before you start out toward your outcome, how will you *know* when you've *got* it? What will tell you? For this to be effective, it is not enough just to "know" it, as if a vague awareness type of knowing will suffice. We need to know it through our senses, and we only have six of those. When you have achieved it, what will it *feel* like? What will it *look* like, to you and to others? Will it have a good *sound*? What other senses will enable you to savour the moment of achievement?

We have no way of interacting with our world, of experiencing our universe, other than through our six senses. We can only either SEE it; HEAR it, FEEL it, SMELL it, TASTE it, or experience it PROPRIOCEPTIVELY, (which is how we know where our parts are without having to see them). For example if you touch your nose with your finger while you have your eyes shut, you are using your proprioceptive ability (and the policeman investigating your sobriety may be suitably impressed!)

Here are some essential features.

Your well-formed outcome must be ***positive.***

It must be within your control.

You need to identify **in advance** *how you will know if, or to what extent you achieve it. Only your senses can tell you.*

*You need to choose firmly in advance, will you elect to be aware of what you **see**, **hear or feel**.*

Choose only one on each trial.

Now would be good time to check over *your* own next desired outcome. Is it really achievable, or is it a bit over-ambitious as yet? Do you really have the time, money, desire, help …. and any other resources you may need in order to bring it about? Does it fit in with the rest of your life, or will it be too disruptive? Is it grand enough? You need to ask these questions, because once you have cleared them, you will feel free to really get stuck in, and "go for it".

Sir John Whitmore (he became involved with the "Inner Game" movement) invented a mnemonic which is quite apposite in this context; he recommended thinking in terms of G.R.O.W which he characterised as –

Goals (what you want) – there is more on good quality goal setting later.

Reality – i.e. where you are now with respect to the goal?

Options – what choices of route toward it, and resources obtainable do you have?

When – when will you start? Have you the **W**ill ?

A little bit of practice. At last here's something to do!

I'm going to ask you to do something very difficult, very challenging and at first seemingly dangerous – and I'm going to suggest you do it in absolute and complete safety! Indeed I'm going to suggest you do it in a nice warm armchair. I want you to choose a time **every day** when you can spare yourself ten minutes. Ten minutes just for you. I want to suggest that you settle down in your favourite chair, and relax in peace and quiet.

You might choose to set a goal of finding these ten-minuteses for say the next single week, and then reviewing. Focus on your breathing for a while, attending to every aspect of it – what it sounds like, what it feels like. Take your time. Give yourself permission to stop everything else for just a short while. You deserve it. If you don't have a quarter of an hour in your life which you could dedicate to this – change your life!

Another practice to do anytime you like.

- I want you to feel your muscles relaxing – first your neck and shoulders, then your arms, then your body, and finally your legs.

- Feel the tension flowing down your arms and legs and out through your fingers and toes.
- Close you eyes if you wish to. Then, I'd like you to (perhaps initially) see yourself skiing. Since this is private, and entirely yours, perhaps you could let yourself "see" you skiing very well, very precisely. You could see yourself skiing like someone you know and respect for their skiing. Let it happen, and take pleasure in seeing *you* skiing just as you would wish.
- And when you are skiing as you would wish, then I'd like you to see yourself skiing faster – still with precision, but more forcefully. See yourself swooping down the piste, your skis cutting through any crud or uneven stuff, and making solid platforms that you can see yourself bracing against as the arcs sweep round. Swoop over rolls, down short steeper pitches, and then open out the arcs on the gentler sections to accelerate even more. Ski like the best skier you've ever seen. Ski like the wind!
- When people play this game they often see themselves as if watching from outside of themselves. In my case I usually see myself as if I'm following myself and watching me. Once you have the skiing established, and you get more practised at this game, I'd like you to find out if you can then let your self move quietly forward toward your fast-disappearing figure and move *into* yourself.
- Become yourself. Re-join your self, and *feel* yourself skiing instead of watching yourself; feel the added speed; listen to your skis hissing through the snow; see the ground ahead of you, as you pick your route and swoop down, arc after arc after arc. Catch the odd glimpse of other skiers watching in admiration. Why not?

It's just a game, and a very pleasant one at that. It's absolutely safe. I'd like to think you'll get very good at it, through regular practice; and when you have made progress with it (if you choose to, and if it pleases you) perhaps you'll later let me have your thoughts on it. Drop me a line at **bobski@bobski.com** We'll do more of this later.

Picabo Street, whom I mentioned earlier, had a shocking crash about five months before the world championships. She broke pretty much everything she had and ended-up in traction in hospital. She only got out three weeks before the championship, complete with atrophied muscles, lack of race practice and all the other handicaps that go with that.

At the championships she won the Gold Medal! Asked afterwards by journalists and fellow competitors how she managed it with no practice, she answered to the contrary that she had had more good quality practice than any of her competitors – indeed she had been doing nothing other than ski for the past three months; hour after hour, day after day.

The only difference was that she had been doing it in her head, while they had been on the slopes, but she'd had more than them. It is now known that athletes who develop this ability to a high standard actually train their nerves and muscles to do what is necessary, as they go through the motions in their heads.

It has now been established that to play this game your brain uses exactly the same areas of itself, and the same programming that it uses for the actual activity. That is why this works. Not only are the appropriate neurological pathways "burned in", but the muscles actually get trained in the correct movements.

Fitness can't be imagined of course, you have to work at it. But if your technique is superb, less strength is needed anyway.

Here's a brief summary.

Never under-estimate the power of your mind and your imagination.

Set up your own well-formed outcomes. A "well formed" outcome is one in which you can clearly imagine all its dimensions with all of your appropriate senses. (Taste is not a good idea for skiing!) What does it look like? What does it feel like? What will it sound like? What will you be saying to yourself as you bring it about?

Make sure they fit the **best** *criteria; we are "making it up" – might as well make it up good! Then use them, as I described above. Practice it. Get good at it. It will re-pay you a thousand times over. It will also give you many hours of real pleasure – how good can life get, skiing whenever you want to? Superbly! Perhaps in a nice warm bath!*

12.

Chapter 12: Control your "self".

More stuff on how to take control of your "Self".

None of the movements we need to make in order to bring about controlled skiing are in any way difficult in themselves. After all they seldom involve anything more complex that flexing a joint, or straightening it. I repeat, you could make these movements when you were two years old.

Skiing is a simple activity, but it is not an easy one. What makes skiing difficult is the fact that it is a so-called risk sport; and there is indeed some risk attached, but in truth not very much. The risks are more perceived than real. Not many of us are stark terrified of actually falling over; after all everybody has done it many many times in our lives and got away with it. We have inbuilt reaction mechanisms for just such eventualities that have been developed over millions of years, and which we have inherited in our genes.

Nevertheless, it is a rare skier of any level of ability who skis without ever feeling apprehension at least some of the time. And this means that the greatest imperative if we want to improve our technique and become more skillful, and even more importantly to enjoy ourselves, is to learn how to control our "selves". Indeed it is an essential; no one can learn when they are frightened. I believe there is a conceptual difference between "ourselves" and our "self". My "self" almost seems like a separate entity from my day-to-day living being.

A key element affecting performance for all of the hundreds of skiers whom I have taught, has been the presence of stressor factors. These come in two forms –

External stressors such as the scraping sounds of snow-boarders behind them, or indeed of their own skis as they cross a change of surface.

And **internally generated stressors** such as expectations of disaster, negative mental images, and thoughts of failure or inadequacy. Or more importantly still, our perceptions of the slope below us. Not the slope itself; the slope is just a slope. What purports to be "reality" is a personal construct. Put two skiers at the top of a slope; for one it may steep, for the other too easy for words. Is it the same slope or not? Nice metaphysical question, but not now if you don't mind.

Way back in the 1960s/70s the English Ski Council introduced a concept for understanding and controlling this aspect; they called it P.E.T. It stands for : –

Perception – **E**motion – **T**echnique. (P.E.T.)

These represent a coupled system, in which each element in a closed loop affects and is affected by each of the others.

Take the example above, characterising a slope as seen from the top. How we *perceive* (P) it, will affect how we *feel* about it (E -our emotions). These in turn will affect our *technique* (T) (Shedden's "movements in motion"), the quality of which will affect the outcome, which will go on to affect our emotions, which will further affect our perception of the circumstances, and so on …..

To the extent that our technique is adversely affected by any negative or fearful feelings, the outcomes will be more or less effective and our skiing might then not feel up to the job. This will then re-enforce our first perception which will further affect our emotions, and so on, and so on. We need to control our "selves" to ensure that our perceptions are realistic and not counter-productive.

What you need to be able to do is generate and sustain an optimal mental state (OMS); to become skillful with techniques which help you to maintain control of your self in difficult situations – or more to the point, situations we *perceive* to be difficult. These include such techniques as really effective positive internal dialogue, and becoming good at imagery; learning how to relax your self is a further specific technique and is not the same as "chilling out on the sofa"; learning how to recognise what is blocking your progress; learning how to handle fear – as Susan Jeffers PhD says, "You can feel the fear, and do it anyway"; and learning how to get the most out of "mistakes"; learning often, to be your own best friend.

Nassim Nicholas Taleb in his book "Antifragile" rather harshly defines what he calls a "loser" as a person who, after making a mistake, does not introspect, does not exploit it, feels embarrassed and defensive rather than enriched with a new piece of information, and tries to explain *why* he made the mistake, rather than moving on. The question is – Do you want to be defined by your mistakes ?

Developing some skill in employing the techniques of controlling your perceptions and your emotions will make a real difference for you in your ability to control both fear, and anxiety. In a sport like skiing which is hampered more perhaps by apprehension than most, skill in these techniques is of at least equal importance to the physical ones.

What is more, if you develop ability with them, you will learn faster and better, and become a better skier than ever you could without them. If you do not "pay your dues" on these topics, and do the work, you will be choosing to end up a lesser skier than you are capable of being. I believe you will be "short changing" yourself.

To become adept at any technique, human beings need to DO them, over and over again. We call it "practice". It probably applies not only to humankind, but to all the animals; I've just been watching some newly fledged robins across the stream and they are "all over the place"; they don't fly well, they don't land well, they don't balance well. These are things they have to practise, just like we do.

It will benefit you hugely to become good at the techniques I'm about to explain. At first you will be clumsy with them, they will seem awkward and you may even feel a little embarrassed using them. You will get better at them, but only if you DO them. Reading about them, and understanding them, will not be enough for them to help you change your skiing and get better control of it. They have to be practised.

Here are some ideas. What matters is making a start.

INTERNAL DIALOGUE: How to stop it blocking your progress.

More than anything else, what we say to ourselves, internally, about our selves makes the difference between good progress, beneficial change, or little or no progress.

For some reason the education system we have developed for ourselves in Britain, and the way we train ourselves socially, mitigate against positive thinking. Time and again my pupils will either make a "mistake" and curse themselves; or do something truly well, and fail to congratulate themselves. Ask yourself – do you really want to define yourself by your mistakes? It will be a nicer day if you don't.

Words are the symbols of our lives. They are the labels we apply to everything. Words are part of our "auditory representational system", and they function not only between us, but internally, to our selves even when not spoken and only thought of. They represent our experiences of our universe. They not only facilitate some communication (far from all of it!), but our use of them structures our perception of our world. They become our "reality".

A cluster of brain cells known as the Reticular Activating System sees to it that when we select one of our representational systems as our preferred one, the others will be sequestered. So if you choose to attend to what you are seeing you will probably not hear anything. Concentrate on what you are hearing and you'll not feel anything. If you are skiing, then while trying to retain in your mind a picture of your ski instructor's demonstration, it is highly unlikely you'll notice what matters, which is what you are *feeling*.

While you have been concentrating on these words I have been using, you have probably not been aware of your chair pressing up on the back of your legs – not until now that is! Now you are aware, because I put it into words.

It is fine to *choose* to attend to the words you hold inside your head, but do remember that while you are doing it, those words will become for a while your entire universe. What you say to your self will define your experience. Your sub-conscious mind (that's the bit that really matters by the way) will accept what you tell it. It is very uncritical; naive. It believes!

Notice in that last paragraph that I put in italics the word choose. No one can make you use the words you keep in your head. Only you. So what you say to your self is entirely within your control; or it can be, if you so choose. If you don't choose, you will be choosing by default to let old habits define what you say to your self. It is not possible not to choose.

You will want from now on to train your self to become aware of the dialogue that goes on inside your head. It will be going on during your activity, and after you stop. It may even start before you begin. Let me give you an example of one of my own that took ages to get rid of.

Whenever I was attempting to ski in powder I would make precisely four "sort of" arcs and then fall over. This happened time and time again, and I was making no progress. Two lots of internal dialogue were going on and eventually I identified them. I came to believe I was a "four…bosh!" Skier. I wasn't scared, just frustrated which got me nowhere.

First, while I was skiing upright and everything was going reasonably, I discovered that I was saying to myself – "This is going surprisingly well; too well in fact, it can't possibly last". So it never did! Once I had fallen over, the next bit of internal g.b.h. began, and to paraphrase, in case the children are reading, it went something like this – "Oh bother, I am a foolish fellow".

You will have spotted my errors I feel sure. My powder skiing development was not the quickest, and you can see why. I was programming myself to fail. By choosing to imagine failure, and then reinforcing it when it occurred I was getting very clever, through repetition, at "being right". It's always reassuring when we're right. Unfortunately it was not getting me what I wanted. I had got too good at what I did.

So I decided to change my dialogue, and you can too. I promise you, if you don't, you will be doing yourself no favours. Once again, this technique is simple, but to make it work you must do it. I changed mine to "I **will** do five, no matter how, no matter what else happens!" Initially I somehow scraped five (just) and then fell over, but that fifth one began to affect my belief, and I began make (slow but eventually successful) powder progress. What I had done was disprove my "Only 4" belief.

The Gambler

The country music singer Kenny Rogers sang a song called "The Gambler". The head coach of the English Rugby Union team used it to tremendous effect to help counter this kind of thinking within the team. Here are some of the words –

> **Every gambler knows, that the secret of survivin',**
> **Is to know what to throw away, and know what to keep.**
> *Kenny Rogers*

And that's the point – you can choose to throw away the unhelpful stuff, and keep the more useful stuff. You are grown up. It is your choice. You may do so. Or not. Be careful to know what's worth keeping ! The negative self talk ain't. Out on the slopes on countless occasions I have had a pupil who skis down to me better than they have ever skied before: arc after arc initiated, ridden, and completed beautifully. One being slightly less good than the others. Then I have asked them how they felt about the run. "Oh! Half way down I was rubbish, I don't know *what* was going on. I'll never be any good".

You've got to know what to throw away, and know what to keep. See any top sports person on TV after not winning a medal. Disappointment yes, but notice how often, before they go off camera, they will have constructed a "positive" to take away with them. This is because it works.

I want you to get a piece of paper and a pen. I want you to allocate just five minutes to relaxing your mind, thinking back to skiing events when things didn't go right, and write down what you find you were saying to yourself about yourself. Read it, and keep it for the time being. Soon you will be getting rid of it.

I'm sure that you can see now, how easy it is for the opening words of our internal dialogues to pre-dispose us toward exactly the results we don't want. As soon as we start talking to our selves with negative phrases we are choosing (nobody makes us do it) to set ourselves up perfectly for disappointing results.

Now I want you to look again at each statement, and select a positive substitute for it. You don't have to even believe it as yet. If you were saying something like "I'll never be able to do this", write down an alternative such as "Can't do it yet, but nothing will stop me in the end: I won't let it".

Happily, you can also see that breaking into these negative loops is not complex; it is simple. But beware, it is not easy. The reason that it is not easy is that we have become very very practiced at the negative, and as you now know – we get good at what we do. Practice makes permanent – well, not quite, fortunately, but certainly not easy to get rid of.

If after reading this you have decided that you will work on your "self" in the way world-class performers do – and they are not different to you and I except perhaps in the choices they make – then we need to help you put a couple of things in place ready.

Let the negatives be their own destroyers.

You will benefit from knowing before it happens, when the negative self talk is likely to start. And you need to know the instant that it does, and for it, itself, to be the cue, the trigger. Then you need a way of interjecting the more effective phrases in its place. To do this you need two additional, and simple, techniques; nothing drastic, nothing hard.

Get a piece of paper, draw a line down to create two columns. In the left hand one identify and write donw the kinds of things you are saying to yourself. Second you must have in place, and practised, ready for use, the replacement phrases and sentences that you are going to use. It's no good hoping they will appear when you need them; they won't, that is when you are under stress already. Write each alternative in the right hand column next to the negative one.

So, for example:

Instead of "I'll never be any good I can only ever do four 'turns' say –

*I'm not a quitter and I'll somehow stay upright for five, **no matter what**!*

Instead of "That was another awful run" say –

From now on I'm not a complainer. What can I learn from that run?

For this to work – and it is well worth the little effort required I promise you – you have to have been practising saying the new things, so that they begin to feel natural to you, and not embarrassing. Remember, at first they won't; what feels natural is what we're used to, and what we are used to is all the negative rubbish.

Ask yourself why you are considering doing this. Is it because you need to be able to help yourself not hinder your self, in the stressful situations? You must have the better phrases all ready for use, or you will be too distracted when the time comes.

Next, you need a way of stopping the negative stuff if it has started. Being able to do this is very confidence building. Different folk use different techniques for this. If you think in images, then as soon as you are aware of the negative self talk you could imagine a brick wall in front of it, which it runs straight into; or you could "see" a red traffic light. If you think in words, you could just say STOP either to yourself or out loud. This last is amazingly effective.

And you need something else to add to these – find a simple physical thing to do as you put your stop technique into effect. In Neuro Linguistic Programming this is known as an "anchor". You could stomp your ski pole into the ground; or knock your knuckles together; or tap your head – whatever would come naturally to you. But make sure you do it, it's important.

Once you've imagined your brick wall, or said "Stop" or whatever, and tapped your head, then you **must say** your new and better phrase. After that, don't hesitate, just get on with it.

I am sure you can see from all this, that what we are doing is working to find ways to ensure that *you* can define and control your own mental attitude at the times when you need a more effective one. Doing these simple things will help you to get the outcomes you are looking for, sooner and more certainly; but do remember that for this to happen you do need to have a clear and defined outcome in your head to start with. If you don't know where you are going, any road will get you there.

You'll also be able to see, I'm sure, that understanding these simple techniques, or believing in them won't win you any prizes. In truth, they're just *too* simple. You just have to do them. That is what works. If you don't believe in them but do them anyway, they still work: it's amazing. Wait a minute, what did I say? I'll say it again – **If you don't believe in them but do them anyway, they still work**. Our words programme our minds.

Go to the trouble of identifying your own negative self talk; write down the key elements of it, and then write down the alternatives you will have ready for the little beggar when it has the cheek to raise its ugly head.

There will be key words that you will find cropping up time and again, and that you can train yourself to use alternatives for. The way to do this is ensure that you have ready and in place before you start, the better alternative words or phrases.

It's not enough to work at not doing something. The best way to stop doing something is to do something else instead. For example, instead of "not having a cigarette", have another behaviour ready to substitute every time you might be about to have one. (Smoke a cigar!) – Easy isn't it?

None of this is going to cost you very much, and who knows, it may not work. Then again it might – it certainly has for a lot of top sports performers, and for me, and for my pupils too. So why not "give it a go" and do it *as if* it is going to work? Then it is quite likely that it will.

13.

Chapter 13: It's the PROCESS that matters, not the outcome.

The importance of Process over Outcome.

"I never thought of it that way – as 'failing'. I kept on campaigning, because it was not down to me entirely whether things changed or not, it was just up to me to keep going; to keep doing the right thing."
This was a monk I once heard on the radio, who had been campaigning on the same issue for years.

All is going well. You are skiing in the sunshine on the kind of piste you enjoy. Lunch is still a pleasant memory, the company convivial.

The slope gradually steepens as it approaches a right-hand bend, but not enough to worry about. Then on the bend it steepens more. There is suddenly a visible precipice to your left. While your attention is distracted by that, the piste narrows and steepens still further. As it completes its bend, rock walls close in on both sides. The sun goes out. There are skiers clutching the side walls in fear. Others below them continue on their way, while their skis do the same but in a different direction.

This is now a complex situation with a lot of factors interacting in a way that will distract you. A mathematician or scientist would describe this as a system with not much "signal" but with an awful lot of "noise". All of the feedback from your now constrained universe has the ability to affect you and your emotions, but much of it is information you neither need nor want. Only the "signal" part of it is of use to you. The "noise" is the rock walls; the skiers below; the sun going out; the once-visible drop that you have now passed but is still in you mind etc.

The looming rock walls will affect your emotions, but the information they offer you is useless. The out of control skiers below you offer the opportunity to tell your self some scary stories, but again are of no use to you. It is time to exercise some "self" control; time to separate the signals from the noise.

You need to **stop**, (Just shout **STOP! – it really helps you)** in safety, and after you have stopped, survey the situation. This *could* give you time to get as frightened as everybody else even though you don't have to. But it also gives you time to review things rationally if you so choose. You need to get the job done first, and be emotional afterwards, not the other way round.

You're going to have to re-start shortly unless you intend to bivouac there for the night. This is where the problem starts. Be aware – what the "reptilian" 40 million year old part of your brain will want to do is to focus very intently on the circumstances (as it perceives them, not as they really are, and including all the "noisy" bits).

The outcome you want – the end-goal, might be the happy result of finding yourself back in the sunshine on the flatter bit four hundred yards farther down. This is all the fast-thinking, instinctive part of your brain can think about; but what *you* need is for the conscious, thinking, rational part of your brain to take over for a while.

Having some ready-made positive phrases and images in your mind, that you have thoughtfully brought with you from the comfort of your armchair back home, will be very handy indeed. How glad are you now that you put in that bit of effort? What will be even more handy will be to stop focusing on all the noise, and also to stop focusing on the *distant* outcome (the end-goal) you hope for, which currently is only a dream goal four hundred yards further down.

You need a more immediate goal to focus on. What you need to do is to concentrate every synapse you have got, on the **process** that will get you your outcome. On the **inputs** that **you** will deliver. What is it **precisely** that you are going to **do** that will ensure the ski grips and "turns" where you want it to? What will **you do** to control it?

Every moment you have given over to practicing your imagery is now about to pay real dividends. Your ultimate goal of safety in the sunshine four hundred yards away is no use to you. It is a dream. What you need now, and what will really work for you is to recognise that your immediate goal – the one that will help – is small, and **simple**. You need first of all to calm down and stop staring wild-eyed at the scariest bit you can find. Find a slightly less scary bit, there will be one. You need to STOP imagining the worst that might happen.

But how? Here's how … After a couple of repetitions your old "reptilian" brain will recognise that neither "fight nor flight" were needed, and your self confidence will begin to return. Welcome it. Congratulate it, and it will stay with you. With each attempt you will "flow" more. "Successes breed successes".This is a practical example of how these things work. They do not work by themselves, they need you to do them.

- You need to pick the **exact** spot on the slope where you will get the ski to bite and change direction. LOOK firmly at that point on the snow. You will not be giving it any choice. You're the boss. It's YOU who will do it.
- Then, give yourself the time to thoroughly image (imagine in detail) exactly what you will do; when you will do it; what it will feel like, and what will then happen. Imagine feeling the front of the ski slicing into the surface to give you that automatically-selected platform that will support you. (More on this very soon). What will you physically **do** to make this happen? Sink onto your flexed ankles? Sink more onto one big toe than the other? You choose.
- The *outcome* will be one arc.
- But only because you focused everything you had on the **process** which **you** would put into effect. That is all you need at present, just one arc. You cannot ski to the bottom right now; all you can do is get your skis to do one arc. And they will. It will suffice. You will not need your skis at this point to do another arc, because you can simply keep that arc going until the ski stops again facing across the slope, so that you can repeat the exercise in the other direction.

You would be wise not to wait until the situation I have just described actually happens. Why not pick a nice gentle easy slope, go to it, *imagine* yourself in this couloir, and imagine yourself getting yourself out of trouble. The more you practice it, the better you'll get.There is no reason whatever why you should not be able to, it is just a matter of wanting to, and practicing, and insisting your brain does what it is told. We have a wonderful brain (well, not me of course but you), but for neither of us did it come with an instruction book.

What Tiger Woods did.

Another way of thinking of this process is to imagine say, Tiger Woods doing what you think of as "Tiger Woods driving off the tee". You see the golf ball disappearing straight as a die some 450 yards down the fairway confirming (you imagine, but wrongly) that what you saw was Tiger Woods "doing a drive". (Bit like "doing a turn").

You didn't. The disappearing ball was the *outcome* of what he did. It was the result of his behaviours. What he *did* was perhaps – pressure the grip slightly more with the right little finger than the left / cock his wrist slightly earlier rather than later / focus on keeping his head still / be aware of how his weight transferred from right foot to left foot, make some allowance for wind direction and strength…… a dozen things that you could never see or feel as he did them. The *result* of all this was a "drive".

In your case, in the scary imagined scenario above, you will relax your muscles / "feel" what your foot is about to feel / imagine your legs first flexing then straightening / "see" your ski tip begin to change direction on the exact spot you identified, and so on. The outcome will be one solid, stable controlled arc, which you will choose either to come to a stop safely across the slope, or choose to flow into the next one.

This is why watching somebody expert doing something is a waste of time if what you are trying to do is learn how to do it. Indeed, watching an expert is the worst thing you can do – better to watch a no-hoper, you will learn more. Woods was not concentrating on the ball sailing away into the far distance; he was concentrating on what he was doing, safe in the knowledge that so long as he did the right things the outcome would be a ball sailing off into the far distance. Straight.

Which is why I cannot play concert piano; I don't know what to do, I could not find out by watching Ashkenazy, and of course I have not practised it.

Here's another philosophical "take" on it; see what you think :-

Skiing improvement, and the extraction of Blackthorn bushes.

With a respectful nod in the direction of my physicist friend Tony, I this morning conducted an experiment.

Having had a number of our hedges and hedgerows laid this summer, we now have a growing problem of Blackthorns encroaching onto the fields. They spread energetically by sending out root suckers just below the surface, off which shoot new Blackthorn plants. This is a very rapid process somewhat akin to the tide in Morecambe Bay; both of them can travel faster than a man can run!

I had the idea that were I to attach a metal hook to a length of rope, in turn attached to the back of the quad bike, I might be able to get the hook around the root and pull up great lengths of it, effortlessly. I am happy to report that the experiment was an unqualified success: the idea did not work at all. The roots proved to be of insufficient strength and simply snapped. I have been constrained to revert to a slower, manual, and rather strenuous process instead. A very satisfactory experiment.

What can we learn from this?

If we don't attempt anything new that we haven't done before, we will never find out what works and what doesn't. Mankind has developed most through trial and error, followed by a bit of refinement of the trials that eventually resulted in the desired outcomes. This is the best way of developing your skiing as well, but with one serious caveat – you don't have enough time to be wasting it on too many unproductive trials.

That's where a bit of good coaching comes in. If nothing else it will help you understand the underlying processes, give you confidence, and help you put both "failures" and "successes" – (Rudyard Kipling's 'two imposters') – in their proper contexts.

Experiment !

Take a light hearted, inquisitive view when trying out something new. Always do it in the easiest, and safest terrain you can find. No matter what actually happens the experiment will be a success. Do everything you can to avoid being too 'outcome oriented'. If you submit to that tyranny you will find yourself classifying everything other than your most desired outcomes as failures. They are not, but you will very soon begin calling yourself names because you don't get exactly what you hoped for. Learn to love *the process.*

It is far more interesting, far less misery-making, if you pick an easy slope, decide on some simple thing you are going to do, and see what happens. If you pick your terrain conservatively it is very unlikely indeed that you will come to any harm, and if you find it impossible to come to terms with even the slightest risk, then reading a book or watching the TV might be better options for you than skiing. But then you wouldn't be the skier you so clearly are.

A further thought on that 'outcome' mullarkey – how rational would it be when contemplating your experiment to expect the outcome to be absolutely terrific straight off? It wouldn't would it? Far more likely would be that you will do something different, and get a hint of a new direction in which your skiing might go, if you develop it further. That ought to make you terrifically joyous.

So – give it some thought, pick the right spot, come up with one single simple thing to do, and give it a go. You may not end up any wiser, but you'll certainly be better informed!

Ideas coming up forthwith in the next chapter.

14.

Chapter 14: At last. THE BIG IDEA

The Big Idea
(How skiing really works)

"To some a cherished myth is still worth more than an unvarnished fact."
Richard Fortey.

Learn how your ski works, and you will be able to make it work, for you.

When we are very young we can readily learn physical activities without needing to understand what is going on. When you learned to ride a bicycle for the first time, you did not need to understand gyroscopic effects, or centripetal force; you just got on with it.

For some reason, when we get older learning in that way doesn't seem to work. At least that has been my own experience and what I believe I see whenever someone adult, educated and let's say middle-aged comes to me for the first time to see if we can enhance their skiing.

Rather, what we need when we are grown up, is to be treated like a grown up and helped to understand what are the underlying processes that make the activity work. It is not enough for some ski teacher to say, "Look, this is what you do – do it like me".

More than anything it has proved to be, on my courses, that it is understanding which enables my pupils to make massive changes in their perceptions and more importantly in their self-belief. Once you truly understand what it is that makes good skiing possible, good practice then becomes possible, and it becomes possible to realise that you will be able to do it too.

Without understanding you will never make much progress in skiing or in anything else. With understanding you can put everything else into context. Understanding is pivotal to progress. It eliminates bewilderment, one the three horrible hurdles.

One of the central tenets of Accelerated Learning is to first uncover "the big idea" of the subject being learned. And the big idea that is the true central core of skiing is known to hardly anybody. It is the opposite of what almost everyone thinks it is. It may surprise you to know that very few people world-wide have ever had put to them the ideas within this chapter.

Scarcely any skiers know it, not even good racers, and very few instructors, of any nationality. What may surprise you even more is that the reason almost no instructors know this, is that their training and authorising bodies appear not to not know it either; not even the official government supported ones, at least in so far at can be divined by what they teach. I have no idea why this is.

To only slightly paraphrase Bill Bryson, in any ski resort in the Alps you could spend a week kissing the bottoms of instructors who know this stuff, and not get chapped lips. In any case a goodly percentage of instructors in ski resorts are "Stagiaires" , only partially-qualified probationers.

I am about to share the secret with you. Up until now it has been known to just a few coaches and ski designers. I owe John Shedden for this. He wrote about it way back in his book "Skilful Skiing". Not many had the wit to see what he was getting at back then (though the Norwegians made his book required reading for their ski teams, and I think still do). Not many yet have the wit. This "big idea" will soon accelerate your progress to a considerably higher standard of skiing. And you will be happier.

Here it comes then – **The Big Secret**, the **Core Idea** – and I make no apologies whatever for giving it this big build-up. Beware of under-valuing this concept; it is absolutely crucial. Take it to bed with you. Sleep on it.

Happily, the technical people who design skis know this secret very well. They have made skis the way they are, precisely so that they will do their job perfectly for you, if you give them the correct simple instructions.

If you learn how skis work, you will know how to make them work.

<u>Here then is the big central idea of what skiing is.</u>

Skiing is a snow *pushing* game.

It is *not* a game of sliding about on snow – that is what "being-out-of-control" is about.

It is snow *pushing* which makes skiing possible: pushing enables you to control both your speed and your direction.

Without pushing, and being pushed back, you are lost; all you will do is slip.

Here's how skis work.

Skis are sophisticated pieces of equipment. They are not "planks", and people who call them such, should know better. Very few recreational skiers have given their skis any real attention, except for the obviously most critical aspect, i.e. to ensure they colour-co-ordinate with the boots! Fewer still have ever had them explained to them.

But understanding them is important because if you have no idea *how* they work, you will never know how to best *make* them work for you, and it's unlikely you will develop confidence in them.

It is basic physics, but you certainly don't need to revise your exam text books; at this level it's really very simple. Very simple, and very powerful. Isaac Newton knew a lot about it, and though his discoveries may not work at the level of sub-particles, they certainly work well enough for us!

The up-turned ski tip.

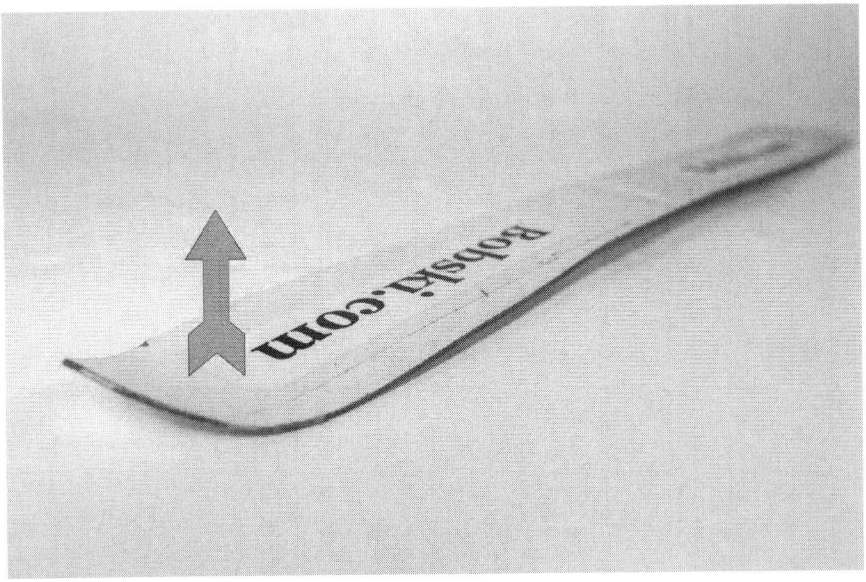

Ski flat – earth's force directly upward

Firstly, consider the ski tip. It is up-turned. Because of this simple feature, when a ski is sliding forward, it is trying to push the snow. The tip meets the oncoming snow and the snow pushes back. Because the tip is up-turned, the resisting snow pushes upwards against the ski as well as trying to push backwards against it. The tip can't "dive-in".

The "push" from the snow acts at right-angles to the sole of the ski. So, in this mode, with the ski flat on the snow, going straight and not describing an arc, the push is mostly upward, with a tiny bit of push backward. It has to be upward like this or the ski would simply sink downwards into the snow; in the same way that the seat you are on must be pushing you upward or you would hit the floor.

The tilted ski.

Now imagine this same ski, heading downhill in the same manner, but now tilted left or right, (not *turned*, just tilted) so that the ski's sole is no longer horizontally flat on the snow surface. Still trying to go straight downhill.

Tilted platform with ski in the snow – earth's push deflects its direction

It can do this because it can distort the snow surface (cut into it) so the snow supporting it provides a wedged platform like that shown here. Tilted.

The process occurring at the tip stays just the same. The snow pushes back against the ski tip, but the direction of this resisting force will no longer be vertically upward; it will be oblique. The force will still try to act at right angles to the sole of the ski, and will result in a combination of upward and sideward push. The sideward component results from the ski responding to the snow's reactive push.

Since the ski cannot just take off skyward, it will instead be deflected sideways from its earlier course, a bit like glancing off a wall would be. Some people call this "turning", but in my view this is a very poor description of what is happening. "Turning" could mean almost anything.

A more informative and useful way of thinking of the process would be to think of it as "being deflected", or as the process develops, "describing an arc", which is like an infinite series of small inter-connected deflections.

All other things being equal, the more the ski is tilted, the more deflection there will be. The greater the deflection force from the snow, the more the ski will tend to bend, and the smaller will be the radius of the arc which develops. The "turn", if you must, will be tighter. This is force dependent; you can imagine how difficult it would be to ski on a very highly tilted ski if you were scarcely moving.

These explanations may not fully satisfy a physics professor, but for our purposes they will do: it is at this level very simple.

The Bending Effect

When you are on the ski, the forces that come into play will do so around your own centre of mass and where it acts through the ski. (Actually, there is a number of centres-of-mass – for example your hands, your head etc., but by managing these bits appropriately the overall effect is for the forces to act through one “aggregated” centre of mass somewhere not far from your navel.

When the ski tip is resisted by the snow, in whatever direction, the force which your own mass exerts on the ski’s centre keeps driving forward because of your inertia. The force of your momentum acts through the centre of the ski, depressing it, whilst the snow pushes back, bending the more flexible and wider tip and tail.

The result is that the ski bends because the tip and tail are more flexible than the centre. The snow’s resistance still acts “at right angles to the sole of the ski” . When the ski’s sole is flat on the snow that will be ‘up’ . When the ski is tilted, “up” will mean something different – it will mean “up at an angle”.

But just tilting on its own, and having an upturned tip, are not enough. If the ski were parallel sided it would still work, but not very well.

When the ski is bent and tilted, the narrow waist allows the whole length of the side of the ski to remain in contact with the snow. Without this ‘sidecut’ only a very small part of the ski would make effective contact with the snow, and the platform would be inferior.

Ski tilted and bent. Sidecut ensures full length contact

You can prove this for yourself if you get a straight-sided ruler, bend it and then tilt it whilst it is in contact with your desk or table.

Straight-sided, the ski would be very unstable. This point is important because as I mention elsewhere, we are not interested in "edges" (I hate the word); what we want are platforms – we need something to resist against. Something for the snow to push back against.

A ski with no side-cut, but bent and tilted, would create a very short and unstable platform which would be capable of moving backwards and forwards along the ski. (The ski would roll about!) Instead, by having side-cut, the ski creates in the snow a full length tilted platform against which you can be supported during the enactment of the arc.

Take a look at this straight-sided ruler. You can see it is like a cheap suit – it only fits where it touches. It touches at just one point anywhere along its length. The tip and the tail are off the ground. The platform it created in the snow would be very unstable. And so would you be. Of course, in snow it would make contact everywhere, but only very lightly at tip and tail and would still be unstable.

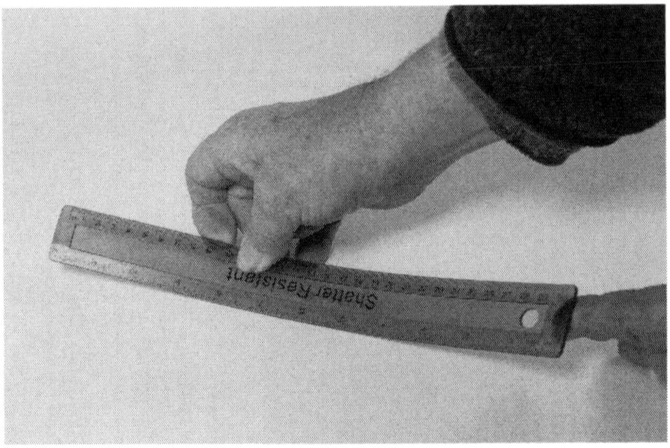

No sidecut, no platform, one contact point = instability

You do not "do turns".

It is easy to visualise that with "side-cut" the whole length of the moving ski is in effective snow contact, and being bent and tilted, then what will happen is the ready description of an arc in the snow. The arcing ski is carrying you around the arc with it. You do not 'do' the "turns"!

What makes the ski describe the arc is Mother Earth herself. When your ski manages (with your help; we'll come to this before long) to find some resistance, then Mother Earth will push against your ski, and because of the design considerations above, that will result in an arc. No "ifs", no "buts". That is what will happen.

You do not have to 'turn the ski', nor even to 'do a turn'. You won't have to slide your feet apart and together or any of that nonsense. With Mother Earth's help you can stay relatively normal and human looking. And you will be the better for it.

You could decide to pivot the ski under your foot, across its line of travel, if you wished, and that might have beneficial effects if you wanted to reduce your speed, or the amount of effort you need to put into your skiing, but you don't need to do it. It is a useful technique to add to your burgeoning compendium, but only when it pleases you, and we shall discuss later when might be appropriate and how to do it.

You could lift one ski off the ground and something else would happen. On occasion it might be beneficial but you don't *have* to do it.

The ski will keep describing its arc, and carrying you around that arc, either until you make a movement which modifies that process, or an external force acts upon it, or until the ski 'runs out of steam' through arcing so far round that it finishes pointing up the hill and loses momentum. If ever you feel unsafe and want to halt the downhill process, just hang on to the arc, ride the ski all the way round and it will come to a stop. Be patient. WAIT.

In effect, because the ski can cut into the snow, and because there is a "side-cut" in its shape, it creates between itself and the snow surface upon which it is riding, a **platform**. It's a tilted platform. It's a platform that you stand against and can be very stable. You are NOT skiing on an edge!

So there you have it; that is how skis work. To make them work, how and when you want them to, you have to make the right small movements, at the right time, in the right way. They are simple movements. I'm going to cover those issues of what to do and when, elsewhere. You will be able to do them. It will take practice with them in order to become skillful in their use. You will enjoy the control you exercise when you do.

A word of reassurance; every one of the movements you need to make, you could make and you were making by the time you were two years old. You do not have to be an athletic phenomenon. (What did I say earlier about my being a perfect example?)

15.

Chapter 15: The three things skis can do.

What do we want the ski to do?

(They can only do three things – slide, skid, or slip)

Now that with Isaac Newton's help we have the Big Idea in place, and we know that our skis will not do anything without an *external* force acting upon them, we need to decide what it is precisely that we would like them to do.

Skis are clever things but they are not that clever; they will do what you want but they don't know what it is you want, and neither does Mother Earth or her little friends the snow flakes. You have to tell them. It has become clear to me that except within very limited parameters neither do most ski instructors, and therefore few of their pupils.

The industry now finds (or anyway seems to believe) that everybody wants to do what the industry calls "carving". All the time. This is so much the industry's belief, allied to its apparent associated belief that we are all about twenty years old and have nothing on our minds but going "higher, steeper, deeper, and faster" that it seems to be all it talks about. Just look at the pictures ! They are "selling the sizzle, not the sausage".

The reality is rather different. What most of us want is to improve our skiing and the sooner the better; to be *safe*; to be able to exercise *control* whenever we want it; and to become truly versatile skillful skiers. Few of us want to be extreme skiers up in the air half the time. We want to be skiers with a portfolio of techniques. Perhaps become the envy of our friends because of the effortless grace of our performance? One day. Maybe.

Shedden, Edwards et. al. identified two clear and distinct strands in skiing. They are manifest in competition on the one hand, and advanced recreational skiing on the other. One is particularly manifest in off-piste and back-country skiing. Neither one is the more desirable; it is just another case of "horses for courses". It is the difference between **Adaptability** and **Versatility**.

For each type of *competition* skiing there will be one optimal technique. One "best". The ski racer's job is to become highly skillful in the employment of that technique and then to develop a high level of *adaptability* in order to be able to adapt that technique to the challenges set by the course designer. A special feature of the course is that it must be, and react, *exactly* the same for each competitor, or the competition would be unfair.

This is why if you watch ski racing, or freestyle, or indeed any other competitive event you will be able to see that every competitor skis in a way scarcely distinguishable from any other competitor, and the differences between them are minute. The winner wins by thousandths of a second. There is only one optimum.

Rather differently, the objective for the motivated recreational skier – you might say her ultimate "dream" goal – could be encapsulated in the French phrase "Toutes Neiges, Tous Terrains". "All snows, all terrains". That is to say, to be able to identify and employ that technique, or combination of techniques which employed skilfully, will facilitate skiing anywhere, at any time, in the conditions prevailing, on a piste or off it. You will need to become skillful in a wide variety of different techniques. This is *versatility.*

You will then not need perfect snow, perfect piste-ing, or even a piste. You will laugh in the face of powder, bumps, and slush. You will push snowballs down the vest of crud, "Sierra Cement", frozen breakable crust ....

Competition requires having one (extremely high quality) tool in your tool bag. "Toutes Neiges, Tous Terrain" requires you to have a very full tool bag indeed, with lots of different tools of different sizes and for different purposes. The requirement is not so much for adaptability as for versatility. And its achievement brings satisfaction and pleasure at least as complete as that of racing well; perhaps more.

What is the ski capable of doing for us?

With your, and Mother Earth's help, your skis are capable of doing the only two things you will want. Just two things.

Firstly, they can slide along their own length in the direction in which they are pointing. When they do this perfectly while describing an arc they are "carving"; when they do it perfectly while in a straight line they are still sliding and it could be either a schuss or a traverse. Take a look at the picture to see what all this means.

I have painted three rows of dots along the underside of my toy ski. (They represent a possible infinity of such rows.) When the ski is *sliding*, each of the red dots in any one of the long rows on the ski's sole will pass over the same snow flake, as the ski travels forward.

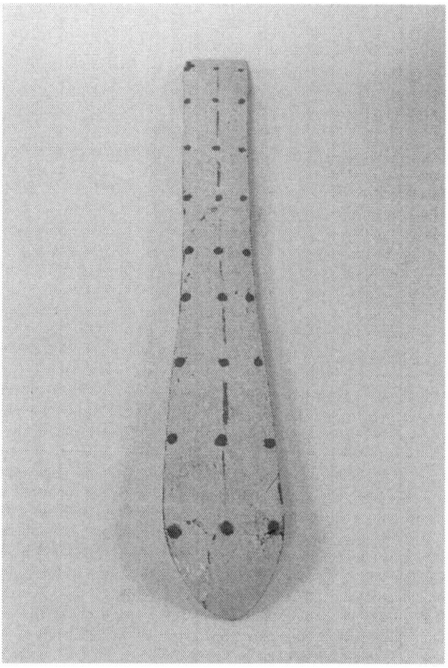

Millions of imaginary rows of dots. When sliding, all dots on one "row" pass over the same snowflake

Secondly they can skid.

A skidding ski will be rotated somewhat across its actual line of travel. It will be presenting more of its side to the snow. Progressing slightly side-ways on. Refer again to the picture. This time each dot will pass over a *different* snow flake because the ski will be rotated slightly across its line of travel. **Provided that it is also tilted,** it will obtain more resistance from the snow and will travel more slowly.

Skidding seems nowadays to be little talked about; indeed some ill-informed folk seem to think it is in some way undesirable. Nothing, absolutely nothing could be further from the truth. The vast majority of us, in the vast majority of instances and certainly off-piste, will need to become highly proficient at skidding. One advantage is that it is a lot less strenuous.

The perfect example of skidding skis, is when skiing in "the snow-plough" conformation – sometimes referred to as "the wedge". In that shape both skis are skidding; both skis are tilted. While you may be skiing in a direct line down the slope, each ski is turned somewhat across it. Each red dot passing over different snow flakes. This creates greater resistance to your progress and reduces your speed. Imagine any snowflake being capable of slowing you down a bit: the more snowflakes you recruit the more you control your speed.

Here's a key "take-away"

"The more snowflakes you recruit, the more control over your speed you obtain."

These two ski behaviours are at each end of a continuum. When the dots all go over one snowflake and the ski is *perfectly* sliding there is virtually no resistance and the ski will not decelerate. If it is also tilted it will bend and "carve" and deliver maximum deflection of direction, with minimal and perhaps even no deceleration. Racers can induce acceleration through the arc. If not tilted it will go straight. Fast. So whenever you want to snake down the mountain without any slowing down, this is for you. Be aware though that higher speeds generate greater forces requiring more muscle strength and endurance.

At the other end of the continuum we would find a "pure" skid. The ski will be oriented at a right-angle to its direction. This would result in no directional deflection, (you'd keep going straight) and maximal deceleration provided it is tilted. It's often referred to as the "hockey stop". You don't change direction at all and you come to a stop pretty quickly.

Key "take-away" summary.

"- Sliding an arc (carving) can give you maximal directional change, minimal speed change.

– Skidding can give you minimal directional change, maximal speed change. (The "hockey stop" is the extreme case)"

These are the two behaviours you want to be able to get your ski to do. You do not want them to do anything else. You certainly don't want them to slip sideways with no resistance; here there be tigers and scary things. It can happen when the ski is rotated across its direction of travel but **not** tilted. Hence my detestation of the instruction " turn your ski! " which is incomplete.

You could usefully think of a *slipping* ski – which is a dangerous thing – as a ski which has not managed to recruit any resistance from Mother Earth; hasn't shaken hands properly with any snowflakes. You'll need to get it tilted and get the tip to cut-in if you want to regain control.

Our objective then, is to be able to slide and skid expertly, in all conditions, in order to achieve the kind of descent we want on that occasion. Usually of course what we will be looking for is a combination, a blend of sliding and skidding. We will seldom want the extreme of either one. Pure sliding on its own gets to be pretty hard work because of the speed and forces that are generated: no one I know wants to do it all day. Skidding on its own won't get you anywhere. Versatile blending is the order of the day.

The reason the best skiers in the world are the best, and I am not, is not because they do something different (and perhaps secret); it is because they do this blending better than I do, in more circumstances, with more predictability. In other words, they are more skillful in the employment of the techniques we need.

There is no such thing as "basics".

I have met countless skiers who's hope is "to get the basics behind me, and get onto the proper stuff". Top skiers have not left "the basics" behind and moved on to some higher secret place only they know. "The basics" are better called the *fundamentals* and they are *never* behind us. The "snow plough" is simply brilliant and not something to leave behind. I'm not saying you must do it all that much, but as Lito Tejada Flores (Instructor trainer at Squaw Valley, and Vail) said "It's the best and safest triangulated experimental platform you can get".

It is also something used very often by expert back-country skiers. My advice? Don't "knock it" and don't lose the ability to do it. One day, being able to do it will save your neck. Skiing as you now know is a "snow-pushing" game: the best thing for pushing snow is a snow plough, especially if you are travelling slowly.

Now don't misunderstand me, I am not advocating always skiing in a snow plough, it is only appropriate for slow speeds. Higher speed skiing even if only moderately so is so joyful, and it **creates** parallel skiing.

The great news about all this is that it means that you and I still have real genuine opportunity to get our skiing much nearer to our dream. The top men and women are not different to us. They are ordinary folk doing something more skilfully. And this applies irrespective of our age or gender so long as we don't suffer any serious physical impediment. Nothing need stop you from getting much better at this skiing game.

Later I will discuss simple things that help you to get your skis to do the only two things you need of them – To **slide**, or to **skid**.

16.

Chapter 16: Don't do Turns.

Turn, Turn, Turn.

"We all know what light is; but it is not easy to ***tell*** *what it is".*

Dr. Johnson.

It is a matter of considerable chagrin to me that in ski schools all over the world instructors are still teaching their tyro pupils that there is "this" sort of turn, and "that" sort of turn, and "another" sort of turn.

First, there is the "snow plough" turn. Then there is the "stem" turn perhaps, where you lift up the inner ski during your "turn" and plonk it down next to the outer ski. Finally you get to do the "parallel" turn, executed with the two skis parallel to one another and not commencing in a wedge format. Apparently not all ski schools do this, but still far too many in my opinion: I see it on snow slopes all the time even now. Why do I object to it? Because it is nonsense. What harm does it do?

It's worst effects are:

- To induce folk to think that skiing in a wedge is somehow the ignominious badge of the complete beginner. Something to be put behind you as soon as possible, when in fact it is a fantastically useful skiing technique worthy of hard work to achieve proficiency.
- The idea of "this" kind of turn, and "that" kind of turn leads many developing skiers to develop ineffective habits. A typical one being to snatchily lift and then replacing the inside ski, in the hope of fooling inexperienced observers into thinking they are "parallel" skiers.

You are wise to dispense with these "turns" ideas, and take on board that skis get *deflected* by outside forces, irrespective of whether they are parallel or wedged.

In any case nobody *is* watching you, they're all too busy. As my mother once advised me catching me gazing at my 16 year old self admiringly in the mirror and preparing to impress the world – "Robert! You wouldn't worry what people think of you if you realised how seldom they do!" A hard woman, my mother.

The fact is, if you cannot create an efficient effective arc when in a snow-plough, you will not be able to do it when "parallel". This is because the requisite interplay between ski and snow is **precisely the same in both instances.** This comes as a great surprise to many people. But I hope not to you because you will have read Chapter 14!

There's nothing wrong with wanting to be an expert, but this particular misunderstanding about "turns" has held back more skiers from achieving expertise than anything else except fear.

Here are the key "take-aways".

There are not different "turns"; there is only the achievement of "flow", which is forward movement, and "resistance" to it offered up by Mother Earth in response to things you do. (Credit: John Shedden). You use your movements to direct that resistance, making it do what you want.

If your skis are in a wedge format, you will be skiing relatively slowly and both will be turned across their direction of travel and tilted. One ski may find slightly more resistance than the other, (we'll come to this in the 'practical' sections) , when it does, and finding more resistance, it will be deflected. It will carry you round in an arc.

It is not a turn, it is a deflection. If you hold onto it you will be granted an arc, which your ski will carry you round. Eventually it will curl uphill and that will control your speed as well.

So what *is* the difference between a snow-plough arc, and the hugely desired "parallel arc"? Answer? SPEED.

You placed your skis in a wedge when you were first learning because you needed to be travelling very slowly. For a beginner, travelling fast is a bad idea. You will be much less wobbly with your feet wider apart and with your skis oriented in a wedge. There is no shame in skiing in a wedge!

But as you get better and more confident you will be willing (indeed will want) to ski faster – indeed once you can do it this takes less effort, but you must be sure you can control whatever might happen. Try skiing fast in a wedge, and you will find it even harder than skiing very slowly, parallel, (which by the way requires a very high level of skill). The wedge is appropriate for slow speed skiing. Parallel is appropriate for faster skiing. But you do not need to *make* your skis go parallel to one another – indeed such is a very poor idea – it will simply happen when the speed is appropriate for it to happen.

In both instances, the reason that the steering ski develops an arc for the ski to carry you around, is exactly the same, in either wedge or parallel. There is not one of kind of 'turn' and another kind of 'turn'. There is just a flexible ski which becomes somewhat tilted, finds resistance to its 'flow', bends to some extent and gets deflected by the external force coming from Mother Earth.

Please don't force it.

Skiing at a speed for which the wedge is more appropriate and then trying to force your skis to be parallel, or 'cheating' them into supposedly looking as if they are, will do no more than lock you into a style of skiing from which you will be unlikely to escape. It will become your destiny. Anyone watching you who is expert at observing will recognise it as not being effective, controlled, advanced skiing. In fact skiing truly "parallel" at very slow speeds requires an extremely well-developed technique. I liken it singers who can sing very simple slow songs, it is far more difficult than singing fast ones with lots of vocal tricks.

So I beg you, cast off any pre-conceptions you may hold about "this" or "that" 'turn' and get yourself onto the right track. If you execute the right movements as you ski in a wedge, then as your speed increases your skis themselves will gradually become less and less broadly wedged. You don't need to do anything about it, at all.

It is the *outside* ski of the arc which is controlling things and it is more effective to focus your attention on that, rather than on lifting and replacing the inner one. When your skis are *ready* to do so they will simply drift themselves into a parallel conformation without you even having to think about it. Elsewhere I cover some of the things for you to physically **do** to enhance this process.

One last observation about "turns". If your perception is that one does a "turn", and then some time later one does another "turn", it implies that in-between the two "turns" something else happens. That "something else" if it isn't a "turn" must needs be a straight line – a "not-a-turn".

A great game to play next time you ski.

Here is a goal for you – on slopes you find easy, aim to eliminate any straight lines of any length at all between successive arcs. Try to notice when one arc "has had enough" and to hold onto it will make you too slow and the next direction change slightly more awkward. Instead, aim to ***immediately****, without hesitation, execute the next arc.*

Be gone straight lines!

You are not controlling much when your skis are going in a straight line, and usually they will accelerate. So it is usually better to work toward linking one arc, immediately you have finished with it, into the next arc in a series of "continuously linked rounded arcs"; snaking your way gracefully down the mountain, like a sinuous meandering mountain stream. A real dream goal.

And for the geography teachers out there, I am aware that streams usually only meander when they get onto the flatter bits. But **we** are mountain people; we ski!

17.

Chapter 17: Ski in Control!

How to get control and how to feel it.

"The only thing worse than a man you can't control is a man you can."
Margo Kaufmann

In the previous chapter I discussed the wedge as an ideal experimental platform for developing new ideas or improving old ones, and also for examining the concepts of flow and resistance as being the way in which skis work.

By first of all achieving an amount of "flow" or forward movement, and then controlling it by obtaining some resistance from Mother Earth, **you** dictate what happens at the interface between the sole of the ski and surface of the snow. It is that interaction which constitutes exercising control of skiing.

Having brought "wedges" and "flow/resistance" together, now might be a great time for me to introduce the simplest and most powerful game for you to play that will embed these in your own skiing.

For the time being you can do it right now in the warmth and comfort of your present surroundings by imagining it, so that when you next get on snow you can not only do it physically, but you will be able prior to moving-off, to remember these imaginings, and you're likely to do it all the better. (Doing it physically, in front of your bedroom mirror is even better). I'll explain it as if you are already on the snow, and *you* can supply the perfect execution of it via your imagination. Don't belittle this idea – it is phenomenally powerful.

First (imagining) pick a very easy, smooth, gentle cleanly-groomed piste. The easier the better, and especially if it has a long gentle run-out. You have rented this for the day, and all other skiers are banned. Furthermore you booked warm sunshine which has been delivered. I don't care that you are already a fantastic skier, pick a slope like this anyway. This is because we're not going to do any "skiing" as such. We're going to have a different goal, and we're going to behave like Tiger Woods in my earlier example, focusing on inputs not outputs.

Our interest is in the **process** and in what we **do** and **feel** as we execute that process. The only outcome which is of any interest to us, is what we notice, and our awareness of that noticing.

To "sell" you on doing this, let me mention Tom Stiansen. Tom won the World Slalom Championship, taking the title off the much showier Alberto Tomba. Tom told me that he used to start every training session by doing this, which is a major reason why I do. The difference is that Tom used to do it with ski boots completely undone! This enhanced his feel for it. Don't you do it though, not to begin with, unless you're feeling pretty confident.

Here is a seriously useful 'game' that I do **every skiing day** using the "snow-plough" as an advanced skiing tool. I don't do it for long, just maybe three or four minutes, but then I have done it a great deal over the years so I am good at it. Nevertheless I would not want to do without it, it sets me up perfectly for all the feelings I'm looking for when I get skiing for real.

Here's the "game".

Pick the *gentlest* bit of slope on the *gentlest* piste you can find. Set your skis into a *snow-plough* that will ensure only a slow forward speed. It doesn't have to be so severe that it hurts your hips (that's why we want the gentlest slope).

- *Make sure your knees and hips are flexed and your back at an angle of forward lean. Especially make sure your ankles are flexed – they won't be if you can't feel your shins pressing the front of your boots. If you can feel your shins but not readily flex your ankles, loosen your boots.*
- *Now imagine that under just one big toe – where it joins your foot and has a little "hollow", there is a little tickly beetle. You want to stop it tickling.*
- *Allow yourself to begin moving, then* ***without leaning over sideways on it*** *flex the ankle of your "beetle" foot ever-so-slightly more than the other, so you can feel a tiny bit more pressure under that big toe, than the other one. You can do this by "sinking" slightly. You can also do it by allowing your chosen ski to slide very slightly backwards relative to the other one.*
- *Do NOTHING more than that. NOTHING. As your skis develop their arc you will be tempted to pivot your torso so that it remains lined-up with your ski tips.* ***It is hugely better not to do this. See if you can allow your skis to deflect away from the line in which your torso is pointing.***
- *Now as you slowly slide forward, simply WAIT.*
- *That ski, (the 'beetle' ski) will begin to dominate, even though both skis are rotated and tilted. It will find slightly more resistance*

than the other. What do you expect will happen? What do you imagine happening?

• *That ski will be slightly more deflected than the other one: it will commence an arc. All you have to do is ride it and it will carry you round.*

• *This is the very essence of your controlling the skiing process from now on. If you're a bit "macho" and playing with "beetles" is below your dignity – DO IT ANYWAY BECAUSE YOU WILL BEGIN TO IMPROVE YOUR SKIING.*

This may seem like a childish game to you. It isn't. When you can do this with precision, and predictability in all conditions, then you'll be a Real Skier.

Once you have got used to these ideas in your armchair or in your bedroom, make this game the first one you play every time you head for the slopes. It need only take a few minutes and believe me it will set you up marvelously for the rest of the morning. Don't forget to do it again after lunch.

18.

Chapter 18: Skiing Stability

How to stand on your skis to ensure stability.

"A thing is right when it tends to preserve integrity, **stability**...." .*Aldo Leopold*

While we are discussing matters physical, and things to be physically doing, it might be a good idea to take a look at how to "manage" our body and limbs in order to make games like the one I've just introduced more effective, and safer.

I was watching the World Championship athletics recently and listening to Michael Johnson discussing the 400 mtrs race, and the 400 mtrs hurdles. I was particularly struck by his attention to the athletes' postures. He was insistent that without an appropriate body posture, performance would be limited – still good but could be better. The athletes' limbs would not be able to function optimally if the posture itself was not optimal. It is a very technical issue.

So it is with our skiing. Don't be put off by the description "technical" – it simply means "to do with technique"; it is perfectly within your compass. The reason that it is of great importance is that when we are skiing we are never actually in balance. Again, there is much talk of "being in balance", and much desire for it, but in truth the kind of "balance" we employ in skiing you might call "fuzzy" balance.

If you stand a brick on end it is "in balance". If you have equal weights on either side of a balance, the system is "in balance". But would you call a Grand Prix racing motorcyclist taking a bend at 98 mph "in balance"? Or a dinghy sailing yachtsman being afflicted by varying winds? No. Rather they are "dynamically balanc**ing**" aren't they? Never quite there, but always ready, actively, for the next adjustment.

Skillful wobbling.

I like to say that skiing is the art of skillful wobbling while descending a snow slope. They call ski racing through the slalom gates, the art of handling a series of linked recoveries! Try to do skiing in ways in which you would handle a static or near-static activity and it won't work. It's like trying to ride a bicycle extremely slowly.

Think of cyclist sprinters on an indoor track. The tactical early part of the race involves jockeying for position, often high up the banking and trying to stand still on the bike, or move incredibly slowly. It's a very unstable business. Yet compare that to how stable they are once they're going fast.

Most of us spend 50 or 51 weeks of the year on level ground, or firm surfaces often with high friction. We are frequently standing still, or moving at no more than a couple of miles and hour. To do this an upright posture is perfectly effective. When we walk, though without realising it or consciously thinking about it, we lean forward very slightly supported by one leg more than the other, get out of balance and swing our spare leg forwards, planting our foot so we spare our noses.

As I've mentioned many times "humans get good at what they do". Ghandi observed that "Our actions become our habits". So our habitual behaviour is to stand upright, with either none or very little flexion at the ankles, knees, and hip joints. These are what folk like me call "the three skiing joints". We all practice this *upright* posture everyday for almost the entire year. It gets to feel like the comfortable "right" one – anything else feels less comfortable, less habitual, and may be perceived as the "wrong" one. That's a shame because the upright one, is the wrong one for skiing. Skiing is dynamic.

An aspect of our upbringing often works against achieving a good skiing posture too – we've been told not to slouch. "Stand up straight, shoulders back, chest out, chin up" all that stuff. Absolutely first rate advice when you want to instill a positive, confident, determined mental state – I highly recommend it when you get frightened. Come to a stop. Shout STOP out loud. Stand still. Do that "shoulders back" stuff, and it works. But notice – only while you are standing still on a level surface.

When you want to SKI again – SLOUCH first, and only then set off.

Here are a few suggestions (even pictures!) to help get a good "Ready for Action Posture".

My little figure in these pictures addresses good skiing posture from the side and with respect to how to flex your ankle, knee, and hip joints.

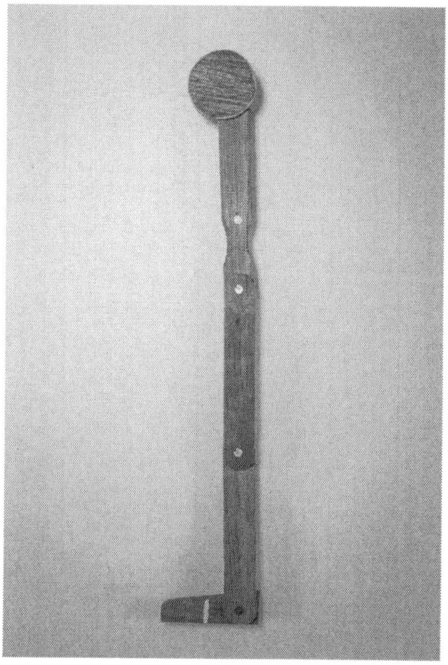

50 weeks of the year posture.

In Fig.1 On our upstanding figure you will see a small white dot somewhere near its navel. That represents its centre of mass, approximately. On its foot you will see a small white line. If you examine your ski boot you will find it has something similar in the same place, probably on the side of the sole plate.

Check your ski and you will find it has a line across its top surface or a mark of some kind between the front and rear binding. Properly fitted the mark on your boot (and on my figurine's foot) will coincide with the mark on the ski. That is the point around which the ski designer designed the ski to work optimally. It is also a key point of reference for where we want our centre of mass to be working through. (All I hope will become clear – stay with me!)

In Figure 1 our little character has his centre of mass behind his white foot-mark and his weight is being supported through his heel. We don't want that when we are skiing. This is far too much like the way a lot of folk ski, and it is hopeless! This is our "all-year-round" habituated posture.

He needs to slouch. (I'm not saying "he" rather than "her" from sexist motives – just look at him!). While this posture is correct if you're on guard outside Buckingham Palace, it is clearly not practical for descending ski slopes. Our skier needs to find some way of getting his centre of mass (or centre of gravity if you like), further forward, ideally over the centre marks on his boots and skis. His 'belly button' white spot would be directly *above* his foot's white line in this instance. But how? (There's more about this on **Bobski.com/blog.)**

Clearly, neither of these next two attempts are likely to be any good at all when you are on the slopes. If you are

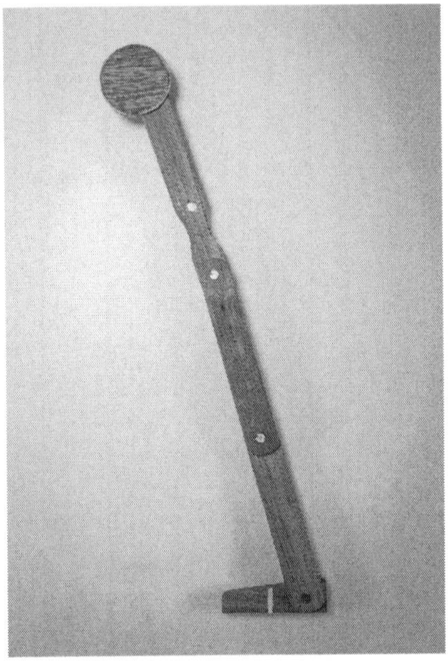

Leaning forward does not work

in any doubt then all you need do is to go to your bedroom mirror, use it to help you adopt either of these, and feel how they would feel if your were skiing.

Rather, we need a shape that will absorb any small bumps and troughs while simultaneously being springy and resilient. We need to develop a posture that enables us to be actively responding to the interplay between the ski and the snow.

Only bend at the waist – no good

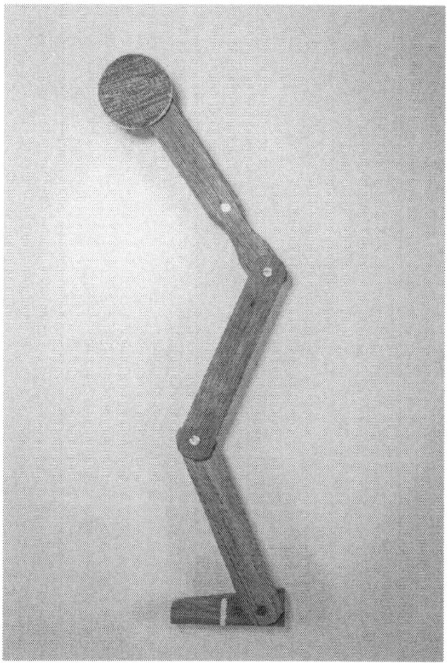

Slight flex (gentle slopes)

For this we need to develop the skill of flexing our ankle, knee and hip joints simultaneously as we ski. The trick here is to do so while keeping "the white dot behind our navel" above the white line on our boot and ski. To do this without rocking forward and backward takes practice – just like it did when you were two years old.

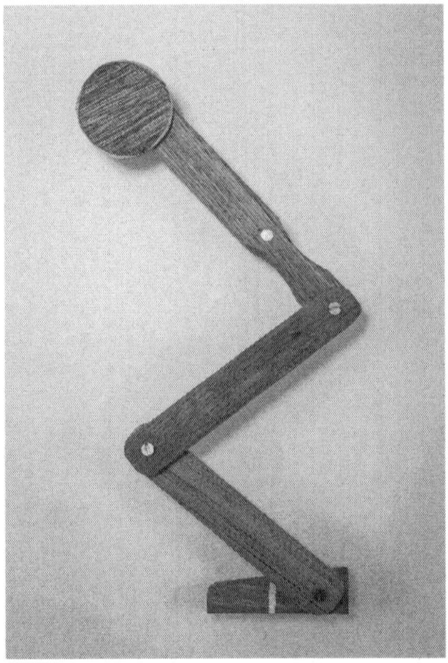

More flex, but centre of gravity stays over ski's centre

The amount of flex we apply will be greater on steeper slopes, on bumpier slopes, and at higher speeds (just look at racers) we will flex most at the *end* of an arc. Press the *other* ski down by extending your leg (not leaning back) to *commence* the new arc. All the time, ensuring the "navel" white dot rises *perpendicularly* up and down *directly* perpendicular to the boot's white line.

All three skiing joints flex at the same time but to different degrees (it's natural enough, you don't have worry about it).

The Key "take-aways"

- *The skier's centre of mass thereby remains crucially* ***in opposition*** *to the line on his foot / boot / ski..*
- *The angle of his back to that of his shins is always roughly the same – if you are as dedicated to improving your skiing as I think you are, then this is a top rate feedback guide for you when you are practicing your posture in your bedroom mirror. Just turn sideways on and check it.*
- *This forward leaning angle of your back (and therefore your torso) is of even more importance when related to the angle of the snow slope you are on. The steeper the slope, the more important it is to angle your torso further forward. And that applies to your shins too. They should be at pretty much the same angles.*

It is this relationship to the slope that is so important. Which is counter-intuitive and one of the considerations that make this simple movement a difficult thing to do when you're on the mountain, because you can easily come to feel that you are leaning down the slope and it must therefore be dangerous. It isn't – it is leaning back **relative to the slope that is dangerous.**

Key "take-aways"

- *You need to give this "leaning back" some thought because it is being* ***relative to the slope*** *that matters.*
- *So, if you are standing upright, relative to horizontal ground like you do most of the year – perpendicular to earth's surface, –* ***but the bit of earth's surface you are on, is sloping away down from you,*** *then relative to the slope you are leaning back!*
- *Give this plenty of thought because it is of enormous importance. Our natural tendency is to stand upright relative to our general surroundings, but it is the* ***slope*** *that matters, not the general surroundings.*

This raises a further and very important issue. One of the features of learning anything at all, is the ability, gradually, to allocate degrees of importance to the manifold elements of whatever is being learned. This one about your back angle is **really important**.

As a result of the way in which thousands of instructors have attempted to teach this part of skiing, a great deal of misunderstanding has arisen. You are not trying to "Bend down, and stand up". Having established the importance of being able while skiing to extend / flex / and then extend our legs again, I now need to stress that while doing this you must prevent your back from rocking back and forth.

What commonly happens is that as you extend or stretch your legs, you inadvertently also allow your back to become vertical each time. You are trying to "Stand up". This is wrong. Often it can be without your realising that it is happening. It is quite unnatural to have your back sloping forward, and to keep it there while your legs bend and straighten. But this is what you need to do.

It isn't a movement you will normally do on a day to day basis, so it is anything but habitual. Guess where is an absolutely brilliant place to get used to it – that's right, bedroom full-length mirror.

I hope you can see that as the joints flex, your torso rises and sinks, away from and toward the ground – it will only be a few centimetres. **But it is a very different picture from "standing up"!** Your torso does not change its orientation to the ground surface.

To "stand up" with your torso becoming vertical or worse, throwing your centre of mass rearward, will be de-stabilising. It will put your mass onto your heels, and your feet could shoot forwards, leading to instability because you are no longer controlling your ski tips – instead you are on their tails. By thinking of each joint flexing appropriately, you can imagine, and you will *feel* your centre of mass remaining above your ski's centre. Then do not rock forward and backward.

If you "stand up" you will throw your centre of mass backwards, which not only delivers poor quality skiing, but can not infrequently be dangerous. This is also why it is extremely important to practice it, especially in the safety of your bedroom (more on this anon). What you will find is that when your back is in its optimum forward lean, – for any given degree of flex at your ankles – it will very likely *feel* as though it is too much.

You are not daily accustomed to it so what may *feel* is wrong, is actually right; and what feels right is wrong – at least for a while. Being able to practice it, safely, and with a first rate method of checking it – nothing more than your mirror – is very welcome indeed. This is because you need to habitually acquaint yourself with what the best postures feel like. You can't see yourself when you're on the slopes.

HERE COMES SOMETHING REALLY IMPORTANT

When I was learning, I was so desperate to "do it right" that when I first came across these postural issues I tried too hard. You might too, so heed this warning. This "triple flexed" posture is NOT a FIXED POSITION.

No matter whether it is flexed a lot or a little, it is not something you adopt at the top of the slope and hold all the way down. The mistake I made, and want you to avoid, was to look at the particular slope, or next part of it, decide how much flex it needed, get into that posture as best I could, and hold it to the bottom. One trainer told me I looked like a cardboard cut-out!

Like so much else in skiing, this ankle / knee / hip flex issue is a "fuzzy" concept. It is unlikely to be exactly the same for two seconds running.

The key thing to remember is that you want your legs to be flexible and flexing. You don't want them stiff, and you don't want them straight – take another glance at Figs 2 & 3. One of the things that holds us back in our skiing development is being afraid to allow our legs to move freely: there's a tendency to want to keep everything still, in the hope of not disturbing the equilibrium!

I like to suggest to my pupils that they ski like Winnie the Pooh's friend Tigger –

> "Tiggers are wonderful things,
> Their tops are made out of rubber,
> And their bottoms are made out of springs!" A.A.Milne

Trying not to move, not to let your legs flex, doesn't work, you need to get used to movement and that's why you must choose easy gentle slopes with plenty of easy run-out. If the slope you're on challenges you, go to another slope when you are working to change, like this: go back to the tougher ones when you are not trying to improve, and are just having fun. No one anxious, improves.

Your standard-issue male for example believes that if you want to get really good at skiing bump-fields (and he can only just get down a short "green" one presently) what you need to do is to find the biggest, steepest one in the resort, select a 'line' down it that picks out the ones about the size of V.W. Beetles, start right at the top and attack it.

This results in a foolhardy chaotic descent inducing considerable UN-learning of anything previously learned, much screaming, a rapid departure from the intended 'line', and sometimes no actual damage to life or limb.

At the bottom no worthwhile recollection is possible because the mind has gone blank, if indeed it wasn't to start with. Nothing will have been learned at all. If you want to get better at bumps, find a short "green" bump run; start two up from the bottom; and if that goes well, next time start three up from the bottom. Anyway, enough of that. What we have looked at so far are practical functional postural issues related to centre of mass, flex angles, and the design centre of your ski.

We are not armless.

We've got arms. (I regret this sounds like a boastful American president).

The content above only addresses what we need to look like from the side, and with respect to our torso and legs. Now we need to address our arms and what is effective use of them.

Whilst we are enjoying the 51 or 50 weeks of the year when we are not skiing we have our arms next to our bodies, and if we're walking we swing them about backwards and forwards. Because we do this such a lot, we get very good at it, don't even have to think about it. It's a habit, and when we go skiing if we don't stop it, it will decide our skiing destiny. Again. Drat it.

When we are skiing, we must move our arms, legs and torsos **much less** than when we are walking or running for example. We do not have to provide the locomotion, gravity does that for us, all we do is stand on our skis and get carried about. The movements we need to make are all small, and subtle. Even slalom racers make small movements. Watching slalom racing makes it look wild and frantic because the speeds and forces are so great; but watch carefully what the skier is actually doing, and you'll find that all her movements are small.

Powerful, but small except when balancing is *lost*. If they get big, it's probably because she has gone out of control.

What we are doing really is learning to adjust to physical disturbances caused by un-evenness in the snow surface, while at the same time simply being carried by our skis around a series of alternating arcs. Big movements are anathema, especially if you are moving at even a moderate speed.

When you are in your car and in the car park you make big movements with your steering wheel, and perhaps your head and shoulders. Do those at 70mph on the motorway and you're dead.

How we employ our arms and hands is surprisingly important. Get your hand carriage wrong when skiing, and everything else will go wrong. Sounds a ridiculous statement I know, but it's true. Glen Plake, once one of the top extreme skiers in the world, said that the instant he couldn't see his hands in his peripheral vision just ahead of his hips, it was too late!

Next, we will consider what our optimum (fuzzy) posture will be when seen head on, and what to do with our arms and hands.

19.

Chapter 19: Arms and hands

How to manage your hands and arms when skiing.

Because skiing is such a dynamic activity involving constant split-second responses to changing circumstances that cannot be controlled by a stream of conscious thought, we have to practice behaviours sufficient for them to become what is known as "autonomic" – things we do not instinctively but habitually.

I attempt to play bass guitar; I'll never be any good because I don't practice enough. For this reason I have to try to think my way through chord sequences, and you can't, there isn't time. So I end up being able to play a few songs satisfactorily, but not all songs. This is an analogy for our skiing: if most of the best behaviours are not habituated we'll only be able to 'play' some kinds of slopes and not others. In those others there will be too much going on too quickly, for us to be able to respond satisfactorily. Hence the frequent outbursts from my professional guitar-playing buddy!

Happily, this is where our bedroom mirror comes in handy again. In addition to giving me the pleasure of admiring my magnificent torso, it gives me and you, the opportunity of inculcating the optimum shapes and postures so they become our habit. As Ghandi observed our habits come to define our destinies. It has lot to do with 'feedback'.

In the last chapter the mirror gave us the visual feedback to accustom ourselves repeatedly with the optimal behaviours regarding our skiing joints and centre of mass. By closing our eyes we could associate the feelings we had with those shapes. Now we can do it for our hands and arms.

I have repeatedly mentioned the importance of small movements. Many of the aspects of the management of our hands and arms concern even smaller movements and positioning. Just like your back, the time comes when what matters about your hands and arms is how they relate to the slope not just to the rest of your body.

Your arms should NOT be held stuck out in front of you. This came as a considerable surprise to most of the folk I have taught. The reason it surprised them is that when they were first learning, some good skier or other kept shouting "Get your hands forward", or something similar. Their hands will likely have been either next to their body, or even behind it without their knowing it. In response they held their arms out in front of them and the shouting stopped. Their skiing won't have improved but at least the mountains became quiet again.

There was a reason for their instructor shouting at them, but this oft-shouted instruction leads to incorrect perceptions because the shouted-at don't know the the reason for the shouting. Invariably, the reason is that as an early or beginner skier they are "sitting back". That is to say, their knees may be flexed but their ankles are not; enough. This puts their centre of mass way behind that magic centre line on the ski, pressurises the tail of the ski instead of the all-important tip, makes your thighs burn like they've been sent to Hell, and renders control all but impossible. Thighs are an excellent feed-back mechanism!

In an attempt to correct this the instructor took a short-cut. But it was the wrong one.

Look again at my little figurine repeated here.

Imagine his arms are by his side. His centre of mass / gravity is already behind the ski's "sweet spot". He is in balance but not over that spot, it is over his heels. Because temporarily he is "in balance" he does not fall over. Now imagine his arms stuck out in front of him. Your arms weigh quite a bit. That weight would now be in front of his point of balance: if he is not to fall on his face he will have to lean his body backward to compensate.

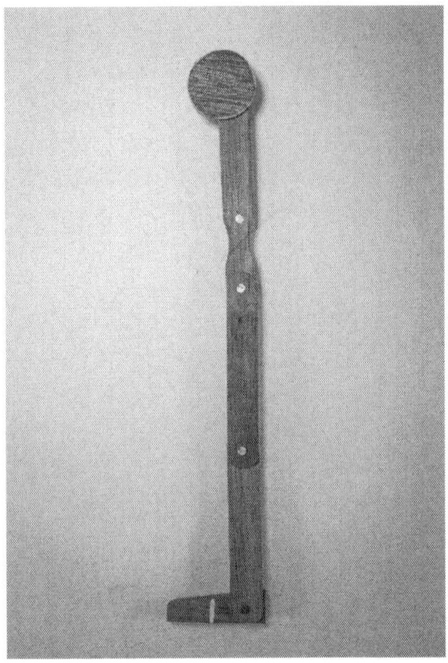

50 weeks of the year posture.

That is the exact opposite of what the instructor wanted and the skier needed. It will not be easy to see but it will happen, and not falling forwards will be achieved only by stressing muscles all over the skier's body as well as leaning backwards somewhat more.

The best carriage for your arms and hands is simply "LOW AND WIDE". Look at Rebecca in the next photo.

Hands LOW, not "forward".

Her hands are indeed ahead of her but only a little. With her ankles, knees and hip joints flexed, and her torso leaning forward down the slope, then if she did nothing but let her arms "dangle", they would be slightly ahead of her torso and her hands would be low. All she has needed to do (because though you can't see it in this photo she is in a mogul field that is steeper than it appears here) is to slightly spread her hands a little wider.

In this posture she is both very stable, and in a position to make all the adjustments she may need. The reason she is not "sat back" is not because of where her arms are, it is because she has appropriately flexed her three "skiing joints", and especially her ankles. Note her left shin compared to her right. This is your ideal ready-for-action position.

A proven and first class analogy for a truly effective hand carriage, is that of "The Hoop". Take a look at the next picture – this is a piece of water pipe that I made into a sort of "hoola-hoop" instead of a pair of ski poles.

"The Hoop" – hands low, wide, only slightly ahead.

Notice whereabouts on the hoop's circumference I'm holding it – about "ten to two" on the "clock face". Also notice that it is lower at the back than at the front. If you look at pictures of anyone skiing fast and well – racers, bump skiers and so on, you will find that you could draw a hoop onto the picture and the skier's hands would be oriented just as they are here. And all because of the posture aspects discussed in the last few pages.

Hold your ski poles like you mean it!

It is extraordinary, and surprising to many folk, that the way you hold your hands and carry your ski poles becomes as important as what you do with your feet. Rewardingly, the best position in which to carry your hands is also the least stressful and the most relaxing. It also facilitates planting your ski pole the most effectively.

I suggest you try this – don't just read it, try it.

Get your ski poles. I leave you to guess where I consider is a very good place indeed to practice this hand carriage. Do it where you will be warm and safe and comfortable and happy to do sufficient repetitions of it until it becomes habitually the way you hold your hands and ski poles. (O.K. Here's a clue; it begins bed**** mirror)

Here's what to do. Adopt a good posture with your skiing joints just very slightly flexed so you are comfortable and your muscles are not working hard. Allow your torso to lean forward in accordance with the amount of flex and the lean of your shins. (You don't have to be in your ski boots by the way, although occasionally that might not be a bad idea). Then simply let your arms "dangle" with no muscle tension at all.

You will find your hands are now *just* ahead of your body. Hold your ski poles by gripping them, but not overly tightly. Please don't hold them between finger and thumb like they are a pair of fountain pens, as so many folk do.

All you need now do, is to have the second joints of your fingers pointing straight down to the floor. Your thumbs will also be pointing toward the floor.

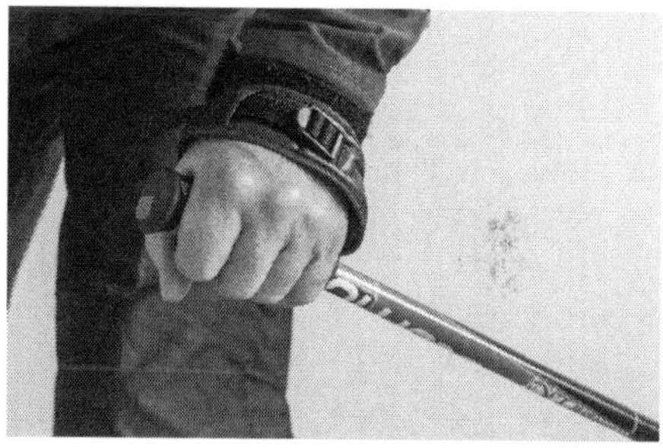

Correct hand grip – your pole is not a pen.

If you are now well relaxed, you will find that your ski poles are probably somewhat below horizontal, and importantly their tips will be *diverging* behind you. Check out my hand in the picture.

These simple but not natural details may seem to you to be a bit "nit-picking". Believe me, they are not. These small aspects of arms, hands, and ski pole carriage make a huge and disproportionate contribution to both how, and how well you will ski. They are not natural, and as in so many aspects of skiing they are counter-intuitive and the opposite of your natural instincts. So they need practicing, habituating.

In the event of some discombobulation when you are skiing, the natural, instinctive response will be to pull your elbows back, clutch your fists to your chest, lift your hands high, and probably pivot your body away from wherever you are headed. Every one of those instinctive responses will make matters worse: quite possible a lot worse. But they are instinctive and will be hard, perhaps impossible to resist unless you have practiced these better responses.

That is why home-sweet-home, and bedroom mirrors are such wonderful training slopes. It is there, that you can practice and habituate all the really useful behaviours that will continue to carry you toward success on your journey to changing the skiing you have got, into the skiing you want.

Whatever you do though, never – never, never, never – work on more than one thing at a time. If you try to short-cut and change two things at once, either they will not change, or they will change but not in the way that you want.

These things are simple, but they sure ain't easy to do when you are on the slopes. You will find them a whole lot easier to do there, if you have done these safe, comfortable practices in the bedroom before you bravely venture into the White Hell that is your favourite ski resort.

One last thought on “ski-pole-holds-man-ship”. You will see many skiers attempting to “plant” their pole too far ahead of them when they are skiing. They reach too far forward with their hand. As soon as the pole is planted, they pull it out again and their arm then swings behind them. This seriously affects their posture and balance. *You do not need to lean forward to plant your ski pole.*

They are able to do this only because they hold their pole like a pen. If you grip the pole handle in a light not tight fist, as in the picture, you will eliminate this and it will help you to keep your body more stable. There is no need to take your pole out again; if you just leave it planted it will come out anyway as you ski past it.

Furthermore, if you do not grip the pole as if you mean it, like in the picture, then your pole will not give you very much support when you need it. Your pole is typically planted just as you are about to change direction from one arc to the next. For a nano-second or two at this time your skis will not be tilted either way. It’s at that brief moment that a bit of proper support is the most welcome.

Becoming skillful at these advanced-skiing techniques is not best achieved when you need them most – i.e. on a 45 degree slope that is knee deep in crud: or even on a black run. So – off to the bedroom with you! And you don’t get your tea until you’ve done your practice.

20.

Chapter 20: Bedroom Mirror

Things to do in the bedroom to improve your ski life.

"…I think one's feelings waste themselves in words, they ought all to be distilled into actions and into actions that bring results."
Florence Nightingale

How you manage your legs, arms, and body when you are skiing is extremely important. Inappropriate posture is one of the key limiters to your progress toward advanced skiing or expert skiing.

In order to control change in anything at all, we need feedback which we can be aware of. Without that we are just "flying blind".

The problem we all have, is that especially while we are actively skiing we cannot possibly see ourselves. So we can very easily indeed, either not know what our posture actually is, or worse we can think that it is something it isn't. We can think it is good when in fact it may be far from it. And we then run the risk of attributing some lack of efficacy to the wrong influence.

Worse still is that about 80% of our brain is allocated to *visual* processing – we are extremely reliant upon it. What we need is some mechanism or process which can help us connect what we *look* like, to what that *feels* like – joining-up the external with the internal. Nothing that I know of is better for this than a full length mirror; other than a good coach, but even they can be disbelieved.

Especially initially, really good skiing postures do not feel at all natural. The right amount of forward lean for your back/torso will likely feel exaggerated. What this implies is that you need to *practice* good skiing postures until they feel natural to you, because they are so different to what you do for 51 weeks of the year.

How to use your mirror to enhance your skiing technique

First let us consider practicing the adoption of different degrees of flexing in your three skiing joints and having your torso inclined forwards. We will address your arms and hands shortly.

Here's a first class practice game.

Stand sideways-on to your mirror. (You can do this in your bare feet, or sometimes in your ski boots if you have your own.)

Take-up a proper skiing posture with any amount of flex you like. Refer to the preceding chapters to check on it. (You'll be practicing flexing both more, and less, as time goes on)

Check that your hip, knee and especially ankles are flexed, and note the angle at which your shins lean forward.

Incline your torso (check out your spine) at the same angle as your shins.

Hold that posture for a few seconds, checking it by glancing sideways at your reflection.

*Now, stop looking in the mirror and look forward as if you were skiing, and **close your eyes**.*

*Your goal is to **feel** what that posture feels like. Let yourself be aware of the sensations in your ankles, your knees, your hips, and your back.*

Then check it out visually again, and repeat. As often as you like.

Then, or next time you do this, change the amounts of flex and repeat all of the above.

*Your overall objective is to learn how to associate good skiing postures with the **feelings** they give you.*

Now you can begin to practice being *really* clever. Practice **flexing more**, so that your centre of mass lowers toward the floor (it will only be a matter of centimetres), and **then extend your legs** so they almost straighten. But here's the rub – make sure your back does not lose its forward lean.

Get used to the feeling of being able to flex your legs and straighten them repeatedly, but without "standing up". Have your torso leaning forward at all times – be looking ahead as if you were skiing – and notice if you back comes upright. It should not.

This in fact is how you will actually ski. You will be constantly adjusting by sinking lower, and then straightening your legs somewhat, only to flex them and sink a little lower again – always with your back inclined forward.

It's not so very different in some ways I suppose, to the old-fashioned business of "bending down and standing hup". Then again, it is **vastly** different, especially in its outcomes for you! That is because your *understandings* of it have now been radically transformed.

And remember, to get to know these feelings you need to check them first, then face straight ahead and close your eyes so you can concentrate on the **feelings**.

This skiing "game" helps you sort-out your leg flexing and so forth. Now let's address your hand and arm carriage. The procedure is the same. Use your full length mirror, but this time re-read the chapter on hand and arm carriage.

Now, here's a "hand carriage" game.

- *First just stand normally, facing the mirror, with your hands loosely dangling by your side.*
- *Next, flex your three skiing joints, and then allow your torso to lean forward appropriately* ***but do not 'do' anything with your arms. Just leave them loose and let your hands and arm muscles relax.*** *You will find that if you really have just allowed your arms to 'dangle', your hands will be* ***just*** *ahead of your hips. That is as far ahead as you want them.*
- *Now, without moving anything else, simply spread your hands a little further apart. For both balancing, and for ski pole planting that is perfect.*
- *Close your eyes, and* ***feel*** *what it is like. Repeat it lots of times.*
- *If you have ski poles of your own, then when (and only when) you have really got good at both of these sets of postural practices, take another read of the hand-carriage chapter, and incorporate those ski-pole-holding issues into your practices.*

When you get on the slopes, you will be SO glad you did these! And all you needed was a full length mirror, in a nice warm room.

21.

Chapter 21: Balance versus balancing

What is "balancing" if it isn't "being in balance"?

"What I dream of is an art of balance"
Henri Matisse (1869-1954)

A central tenet of my coaching is that it is *understanding* that lays the best foundation for you to make the changes to your skiing that you want to make. Attempting to make those changes by just "getting the miles in" is a fruitless enterprise. I have already hinted at a difficulty in this regard that is created by a misunderstanding of what "balance" means in the context of skiing.

At the un-named but miserable plastic slope I attended for years, my instructors frequently advised me that I was not doing well because "…*you don't ski centred and balanced*". They never explained what this meant or how it was to be done. Here is a picture of "*centred and balanced*".

Completely in balance !

We spend a great deal of our year standing upright on a horizontal surface. When standing still we are "in balance"; (actually we are constantly adjusting our position in order to stay upright be we are not consciously aware of doing so). This brick is "in balance". We don't want to ski like a brick.

There is a large number of dictionary definitions of "balance". The most useful ones for us as skiers include – "Physical equipoise"; and (oddly at first sight), "An equality between the two sides of an account". I'll come to that in moment. Equipoise is defined as "**A counterpoise; an equivalent force**". This exactly sums up what balancing whilst skiing comprises. In fact it is what standing upright on a horizontal surface comprises as well, but we do not usually think of it in this way.

To comprehend how skiing is achieved we need to get this idea of "equipoise" and **forces in opposition** into our heads.

Forces in opposition

Our brick is exerting a force downwards because of gravity. The surface it is standing on must be exerting a similar force upwards or the brick would fall through. If the surface exerted more force than the brick it would take off. Isaac Newton – go to the top of the class!

BalancING, not "in balance"

Now take another look at Rebecca. Especially look at her right hand ski. Take note of the snow under her right foot being squashed and displaced (it applies to the whole ski but for now let's concentrate on where her foot is.)

You can actually *see* that she is having to use the muscles in her right leg to brace her foot against the snow in order to not slip sideways. Voila! "Physical equipoise – an equivalent force". There is an invisible force coming obliquely up from the snow surface – from Mother Earth – which is perfectly balanced against the force her ski is delivering. She is ensuring that force goes up through her leg and through her centre of mass by keeping the ski tilted. This is **exactly** what that earlier picture of the tilted model ski showed us.

She does this by ensuring her centre of mass is both lowered toward the ground by flexing, and kept *inside* the arc – nearer to the centre of the circle of which the arc is a part. The two sides of the "account" are equal. And the result is an ARC described in the snow by the ski.

This is what we choose to call dynamic balancing. It is unlike the brick because she constantly has to make small movements whilst in motion, in order to maintain her equilibrium. It is equilibrium she's seeking, not "being in balance", which is an idea that translates into an unwillingness to allow yourself to be anywhere other than directly above your skis, as if you were walking down the high street.

Balancing is what you have been doing all along when you skied, but without perhaps realising what has been going on. Re-assuring to find out, isn't it?

It is the forces coming up off the snow, working initially at the ski's tip and then as you can see above, all along the ski's length, which give it direction. The force under the brick is vertically upwards, the force under Rebecca's skis is obliquely upwards so they are describing an arc as the ski is constantly deflected in one direction until she wishes to change it to the other. That will require some movements shortly, to induce the skis to tilt the other way.

All of this is being done on an uneven surface, which will also have different amounts of resistance – some softer snow, some harder – and while skiing at some speed. A well developed ability to keep the forces precisely opposed is needed, and to do it requires managing our legs, body, arms, head etc effectively, and this in turn is best achieved with our "Ready-for-Action" posture as described earlier.

So in one sense we are never "in balance" in the way the brick is, and in another we are constantly "balancing" which requires a certain agility and cannot be achieved by keeping our body, legs etc un-moving. Balancing is the constant readjusting of ourselves in order to keep the forces developed by our motion **in opposition** one against the other.

An extreme example of how this works is the so-called motor-cycle "wall of death" that we used to see at fairgrounds. The walls of the circle are vertical, and yet because the bike rider gets up enough speed, they are able to ride round on the vertical walls, while they and the bike are horizontal! This is simply through achieving sufficient speed, and to exactly oppose one force against the other. – The bike pushes the wall, the wall pushes the bike. It's exactly like the brick, but as if the brick were standing horizontally. Or like a ski pushing snow.

To ride the bike on the vertical part of the wall needs a certain speed to be achieved. At the bottom of the wall there is a 45° section for which not as much speed is required to maintain equilibrium, and of course on the floor equilibrium can be achieved even standing still; although that is not easy on a bike it can be done.

The same applies to your skiing. Skiing very slowly you can be more upright, skiing fast in an arc you need to be bracing your foot much more laterally as in the picture; **against** a tilted platform. First achieve some movement, then find some resistance. This is balancing, and skiing – one force against another. It's a pushing game.

Here's the most instructive pushing game ever devised. Practice this when you are on a gentle slope until you are really versatile at it, and you will have embedded all of the key elements of control that you will ever need.

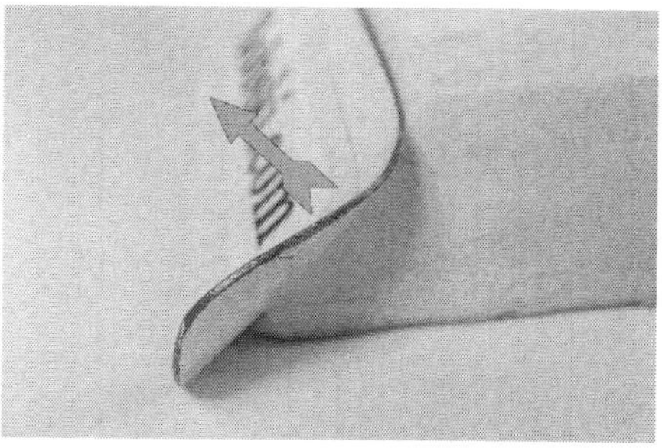

Tilted platform with ski in snow – earth's push deflects its direction

In this image we see a tilted left hand ski approaching us . We cannot see the skier's right hand ski, but that is of no importance because this ski is the one controlling the arc. The force coming up off Mother Earth is acting at right-angles to the ski's upper surface – at right-angles to the face of the wedge representing the tilted platform the snow would provide. The force is not vertically upwards from the floor. It is pushing the ski towards *its* right, (our left as we look at it) creating a right hard arc.

Here's the game one more time:

Yet again your bedroom or sitting room is an ideal place to get the idea before your transfer it to the snow.

- *Get yourself into your best "ready-for-action" position, with your feet placed as if for a gentle "snow plough". Imagine your feet in their boots attached to the ski. You are bracing your legs and boots in direct opposition to the force coming up from beneath the skis.*
  Consider your left ski, as above.
- *The nearest bit of you to that important part of the ski, is your left big toe. You want to control the side of the ski tip, circled; the bit of your foot around your big toe is the best thing to do it with. Learn a simple way of using that, and you are well on the way to exercising skilful controlled skiing.*
- *Here it is, in a simple almost child-like game. Underneath where your big toe joins your foot, there is a little hollow. Feel where it is.*
  Imagine a little harmless beetle in that hollow. Imagine it tickling a bit, and you want to stop it. You want to press on the beetle without killing it.
- *The way to do this is to very slightly flex your LEFT ankle more than your right. You must do this* ***without leaning over*** *– keep your body central between your feet, and facing*

forward. Avoid twisting. As soon as you sink very slightly more on -in this case your left "beetle" – that ski will take control. Mother Earth will push up just a tiny bit more under that ski tip than the other because you are pushing her just a tiny bit more. (She's got a lot more push than you).

- *This will give that ski priority. It will be deflected, as hinted in the photo, to its right. And it will carry you with it around to your right.*

This may seem a silly game to you. It certainly seems so to many ski instructors, I presume because it is not sufficiently 'macho' or 'technical'. They are reluctant to employ it. This is a pity because it is easy to understand, easy to practice, and extremely effective.

An internationally renowned racing coach of my acquaintance tells me that the most frequently repeated command even to top quality racers while training, is "Get onto the tips more!" When they do, they are doing no more than "squashing beetles". I absolutely guarantee to you that if you become well practiced at this little game you need *never* find yourself out of control.

I have more games that take you further but it's on the slopes that we need to practice those.

22.

Chapter 22: Banish "edges" !

Skiing's most reassuring revelation!

"You can't ski on an edge"
Bob Trueman

Platforms. Not 'edges'

Skiers seem to love "edges", or claim they do. They talk about them all the time. The need to have them razor sharp (hardly ever actually, probably never for recreational skiing).

The supposed need to *"get them on their edges"*. Remarks from TV commentators about *"getting an earlier edge"*. Crashes caused by *"catching an edge"*. It is interminable. It is taught everywhere; talked over in bars everywhere; never questioned anywhere; and has become a meme that folk buy into in order to be one of the in-crowd. It sounds quite "skier-ish"; instructors love it. And I upset a lot of folk by saying this – **it is also complete and utter nonsense.**

And it is not good teaching. I don't say this to be contrary. Obviously skis *have* edges, in so far as they are not infinitely wide. Also obviously, since they have to incise the snow surface they have to be sharp enough to do so. Normally, because the surface most of us ski on most of the time is not bullet proof ice, like it is for slalom racers, we do not need the edges incredibly sharp.

If we skied on edges, a pair of machetes would be the ultimate pair of skis: they have got wondrous edges.

But here is the important point – **it is impossible to ski 'on an edge'**. You may find the following pedantic at first, but bear with me; you will be the better for it.

I frequently ask my pupils to conduct a thought experiment. Clear your mind and in a moment I'm going to say two words. I'm going to leave a brief interval between speaking each of them. I want you to do nothing more than find out if you can become aware of any internal, perhaps vague **feelings** as I say them. Your goal is simply to hear the word and **be aware of any feelings** somewhere inside you. No thinking please, just awareness.

First word coming up …

EDGE!

Close your eyes. Any feelings you can become aware of ?

Second word coming up …

PLATFORM

Close your eyes. Again, any internal feelings ?

Only one person out of hundreds ever expressed a preference over their feelings when I said "platform", for the feelings they felt when I said 'edge'. It turned out they had misunderstood anyway.

Edges are sharp. They cut. They are narrow. Being on one feels unstable. Mental images of nothing either side, long drops, and imminent danger are common. No one likes them. It would be fine to keep talking about them if they did like them.

Platforms on the other hand are seen as safe. They are. Often wide. Stable. Not scary. Standing on a platform is quite nice to contemplate. So if skiing were to do with nice safe platforms it would be welcome, and pleasing to know it. **It is.**

It might lead to easier learning. I have news for you. **It does.**

It's so bracing !

Take yet another look at Rebecca. You could say, if you wanted to, that she has her skis "on their edges". But it would be a very poor description of what is happening. You only have to look at the soles of her skis so see what is happening.

Namely, that because her skis are within the snow, and because there is an equipoise between the force coming up from Mother Earth and of her resisting that force, and because the skis have a side cut, a **platform** is automatically created in the snow along the full length of her skis. All she needed to do was to ensure they tilted; she didn't "get them on an edge".

It is bracing against that **platform** that gives her stability, not "skiing on an edge". It will give you stability as well.

There are all sorts of good things about skiing platforms. The obvious one – you wouldn't be able to ski without them;

Key "take-aways".

- *Platforms are wide and stable unlike edges which are simply points where there used to be something and now there isn't.*
- *Platforms are automatically created (sometimes tilted for you, sometimes not, if the skis are flat on the snow).*
- *Platforms progress along with you wherever you go – a little bit like the Heffalump traps that Winnie the Pooh wanted to put just in front of where a Heffalump might be if it came along, and might want to take its next step. Platforms are always there.*
- *And even better, the size that the platform needs to be in order for you to be able to brace against it, is* ***automatically selected by the interaction between the ski and the particular bit of surface you are on at the time.***

You now know that you cannot ski at all unless Mother Earth is pushing against your skis, in the same way that you could not stand up if she did not push up against the soles of your shoes. How much would she have to push *against*, if all she had available was the *edge* of one of the machetes I spoke of ?

I find this ability of the ski to create a platform of exactly the right size almost magical. It happens because of the density – and therefore the strength – of the surface at any given point. In the photo of Rebecca the snow is soft enough for the skis to incise into it sufficiently to provide a platform the width and length of the ski.

If the snow were softer, the ski would sink further in. If it was powder snow it would be so soft that Rebecca would need to place her skis closely next to one another to make them something like a snow board. Mother Earth would then have a lot more "purchase" and the platform would then support her. How much use would an edge be, then?

At the opposite end of this continuum, if the surface was ice, (and then she *would* need very sharp edges) the ski would incise the surface only very little. It's a hard surface. A strong surface. It might then make a platform, say, only one millimetre wide. Because of the genius of side cut it could still be the whole length of the ski.

But here is the brilliant thing – that 1mm platform could have all the strength needed – because ice is so much stronger than powder, or of the snow shown in the picture. It would have all the strength of the platforms you can see there, maybe more. So she would be able to brace against it.

Once you have developed the ability to skillfully induce your ski to **tilt,** and present its tip to the snow, you need do nothing in most circumstances (powder snow being a case in point) that will differ from surface to surface, other than by degree. When you learn how to tilt your skis, and come to trust the *platform* that your skis and Mother Earth automatically create for you, you can rely on them creating the right platform to suit the circumstances. One thing less to think about.

And the other plus ? You can stay away from edges; few folk like being too near the edge.

23.

Chapter 23: Exchange is no robbery.

S.W.A.P Your Skiing

"Life is a reciprocal exchange. To move forward you have to give back."
Oprah Winfrey (1954-)

You want to S.W.A.P something about your skiing that you don't very much want, in exchange (or perhaps in addition!) for something you do. You will not lose in the exchange. In fact you do not have to "throw the baby out with the bathwater".

For example, if you have a way of somehow or other getting yourself down a piece of piste you wish you were not on, and while it may not be pretty it has proved effective – **keep it**. Don't be too quick to want to get rid of it. When you have added a better way, you will then have two ways. 100% profit!

What do I mean by SWAP ? By this I mean always **S**ki **W**ith **A** **P**urpose. It is all too easy to ski with your mind "in neutral".

Perhaps some people can do that but I certainly can't when I want my skiing to be any good. I need to have a single focus on something. It doesn't have to be anything immensely significant, but the potential for things to "go to pot" increases enormously if I have not made up my mind up **before setting off** about some one single thing that I am going to allow myself to be aware of as I ski. I need focus.

This is the thing I will review, albeit briefly, when I come to a stop. Just to investigate it out of interest. Here are some examples of things you could choose to focus on over the next 300 metres (not more). I strongly advise not skiing huge lengths of piste when you want to begin bringing about worthwhile changes: short stretches with stops for contemplation work so much better. Do some skiing later.

Remember, you are not trying to "SKI" at the moment, you are just going to work on one simple thing. (A bit like Tiger Woods practising his hand-hold on his club: when practicing, his only interest in where the ball went is in what that told him about how good his hand-hold was).

Here are a few examples from many, that you could choose:

Learning Objectives.

- *Before you move off get into and check your ready-for-action posture.*
- *Decide which single aspect of it you will focus on over the next short stretch. You have plenty of choice, but must only choose ONE thing. Ankle flex? Back lean? Arm carriage? Where are your knuckles pointing? Have you got a "hoop"? Are you holding your poles like fountain pens? The only thing that makes any of this complex is trying to do more than one at once. Otherwise it's simple.*
- *Let yourself be aware of the "beetle" I referred to earlier – again before you set off, and keep that focus on every change of direction you make, by sinking onto it as the arc develops.*
- *Experiment with flexing your ankles, knees and hips a little more, then a little less so that your body rises and falls just a little, and feel your back being constantly forward-leaning as you do it. Get used to the sensations.*
- *Again, before you start moving, focus your attention on that little spot by the ski tip that you are going to want to cut into the snow (see the picture on page 129). Imagine yourself using that like a wood-carver would use a gouging chisel to incise an arc in a piece of wood. Imagine yourself sinking onto your "beetle" so that spot on the tip cuts into the snow and the snow pushes it round into an arc that you will ride. Just ONE arc so you get the feel of it.*

Some of these suggestions may be confusing. I am sorry about that but cannot think of a way of avoiding it. The best way to do these and other developmental practices is on the slopes and we would need to be together to do that.

But even though they are perhaps confusing just at present, the key factor in this is that by **S**kiing **W**ith **A P**urpose, no matter how you do it, you will be developing perhaps the most important ability of all and that is to become aware as you ski, of **what** you *feel*, **when** you *feel* it, and **with what** those *feelings* are associated. What are your skis telling you?

Stick to VERY gentle slopes when you are doing these things. It's not a matter of "pride" or "challenge" or "keeping up with the others". Once you have developed a sense of "feel" and "awareness" you will have something of great value that only an extremely small number of skiers ever develop, and it will take you far. Perhaps I'll meet you there, if I can catch up with you.

Whatever else you do, I only ask you to enjoy the *process*. Skiing is marvellous isn't it? Perhaps we'll meet on a slope somewhere.

Appendix

Misleading Instructions

You have read of my distaste for many of the instructions too often given to skiers. Here is a brief recap of a few of them, with a short explanation of why they mislead you.

Bad instruction # 1: "Bend your knees".

Quite correct; you can't ski unless your knee joints are flexed. But in the circumstances in which this instruction is usually given your knee joints are not the critical issue – your ankle joints are. The instruction is usually given because the skier is standing too starchily upright with stiff legs. Try this and you will find it extremely unstable feeling.

The instruction is intended to induce you to have flexible legs, which is fine, but because your attention is directed to your knees, it tends to lead to a flexing of the knee joint to the exclusion of your ankle joint. This is compounded by boots that are too stiff.

This leads to your bottom sticking out rear-wards, and your shins remaining vertical, thereby putting your centre of mass so far back that your thigh muscles will be over worked trying to stop you falling over.

A far better instruction would be "Flex your ankles so that you sink a little *lower* toward the ground". You will automatically flex your knees if you do this. Your centre of mass will remain over the ski's sweet spot and you will be more stable.

Bad instruction #2: "Carry your hands forward !"

Having given the "knees" instruction, which you obeyed, your instructor now notices that you are sat slightly back. Your centre of mass is behind the ski's centre but not so much that your thigh muscles are unable to hold you upright. "Carry your hands forward" comes the cry. But the more weight you carry forward, and the further forward you carry it, the **more** you have to lean back. Try holding a tray in front of you with a couple of heavy-ish items on it. Try it first with them near the leading edge, and then try it with them on the back edge close to you. You'll see what I mean. Better still, you'll *feel* what I mean.

Think back to my "stick" man, and ask yourself is your centre of mass above the centre of your foot. No. So the difficulties are compounded. You have to squat and put some of your weight behind that centre, simply **because** the weight of your arms is so far ahead of you that you would fall over backwards otherwise.

The more you do one, the more you have to do the other and matters rapidly go from bad to worse. What is even more regrettable is that you are now practicing a series of behaviours that will *inhibit* your progress toward skillful skiing. (i.e. you will be getting good at it and making it more permanent)

Bad instruction # 3: "Sit down: Stand Hup!"

Two less than desirable behaviours having now been introduced, and desirous of helping you become more active on your skis, your instructor now tells you to stand up and sit down.

Again, this is well intended. It is an instruction with its feet steeped in history, back to the times when skis would hardly bend at all. To get them to change direction you had to virtually jump into the air, pivot them, and land back down in a new direction. Times have changed.

You have by now been told to bend at the knees, and stick your arms out in front of you. Now you have to sit down , and then straighten your knees. It will be difficult.

It will also be unpleasantly ineffective. This is partly because you will inevitably rock your body alternately forwards and backwards which will throw your weight forwards and backwards as well. This will be de-stabilising and your skis will not be doing what you want them to do, which is to change direction.

In order to work effectively for you, your skis need to be meeting resistance from Mother Earth. You are not going to get any if your skis are not in contact with her. What you **really** need to be achieving – only briefly – is greater resistance; greater pressure between ski and snow.

"Standing hup!" extends your legs; in itself not a bad thing. This might help achieve a brief increase in contact pressure between ski and snow, **but the reason you are doing it is <u>to push your skis *down*, NOT lift you *up*</u>**. It is a very different concept, and once accepted is likely to help you retain your back lean. Thinking of "standing hup" will almost certainly lead to throwing yourself up and **back** into a "standing to attention" posture.

Instead, provided you understand that the intention is to attempt, however slightly (and it need not be much), to push your skis down onto the snow more firmly, you will be able to teach yourself to flex and extend your legs **without losing the forward lean of your torso.**

"Sitting and standing hup!" leads to the next bad instruction …

Bad instruction # 4: "Turn your skis!"

This is another one with a hint of truth in it, but not enough by itself. If you rotate your skis across your line of travel they *might* change direction. It does not necessarily follow. If they are in the wedge configuration and you rotate one of them rather more than the other, it probably *will* do that because it will also be tilted .

If it isn't tilted, all it will do is slip sideways. A half-correct idea has been implanted in your mind. If your instructor sees that "turning" your ski is not working for you, and you are achieving only a "sketchy" vague direction change, he or she may well then offer you yet another misleading instruction –

Bad instruction # 5 : " Transfer your weight across" / "Lean over your outside ski"

(I watched numerous instructors only this year, telling skiers this, and demonstrating it. It was an unpleasant experience.)

Imagine you have pivoted your right ski in the hope of steering leftward but nothing much is happening. You have obtained insufficient resistance from Mother Earth, and you need more.

The best way to achieve it is by tilting the ski; toward its left. Remember the ski tip pictures earlier where the inner part of the tip incises the snow surface. Your instructor however tells you to lean over your right ski – to lean over sideways.

The result of this leaning regrettably may be a partial success. Regrettable because it reinforces both your and your instructor's belief that this is a good thing to do. But it isn't; it is one of the many factors that stick you on the dreaded "plateau" of so-so skiing where most skiers live.

The reason is that you need your ski to be tilted towards the direction you want to go. This will give a solid platform in the snow for your ski to obtain resistance. (Take a look at Rebecca's picture again). But if you lean over onto it by transferring your weight across, you will flatten it onto the snow. It will lose its tilt, and you will lose your platform. Later, if you go on to more difficult terrain it can actually be dangerous.

The only reason it changes direction at all if it does – and it won't be much – is because the slight increase in pressure between ski and snow adds a small bit of resistance because more snowflakes are recruited. On very easy slopes, at very slow speeds you will get away with it, which is a great pity. Everything you "get away with" on very easy slopes gets embedded as a habit. If those habits are not appropriate as you progress, the day will come when they bite you. In this case that is when you slightly overdo it and the **outside** edge "catches" ; the ski suddenly stops and then you will crash and 'high-side' it.

It is a terrible instruction, and it is still frequently taught. At the end of your lessons when your instructor skis away for his cup of coffee or schnapps, if you watch carefully you will find he doesn't do any leaning over onto the outside ski at all. Why should you?

All these instructions set you up very badly for your pursuit of mastery of skiing. They have helped holiday makers to convert from being totally unable to ski to being able to 'kind of' do it on the beginner slopes. Beyond that, by having inculcated incorrect understandings they have misled you. It does not need to be like this, proper understanding can be developed from the very start.

The Author:

After some time in the services Bob Trueman tried a number of jobs repeatedly discovering somewhat later than each employer that he is unemployable. Instead he started a manufacturing company which he grew to No.2 in the UK and No.1 in Europe.

He has been a fanatical rock-climber, mountaineer, trans-Atlantic sailor, lecturer, copy-writer, business consultant, historic lifeboat coxswain, and far too much besides. He is a rubbish bass-guitar player and is now an old man.

None of which matters. What matters is that he took up skiing late, at age 46, went to lots of ski schools and by age 54 was no better than when he started. Then he chanced upon a good coach who helped him change his skiing beliefs. He trained first to become a dry-slope instructor, then an alpine instructor, and finally an internationally qualified coach and instructor tutor.

He proved you don't have to be young (makes it easier), you don't have to be an athlete, and your gender doesn't matter. By falling into every learning hole and horrible hurdle you are likely to encounter on your skiing journey, he has helped many hundreds of pupils to avoid them.

He believes you have good reason to trust in your self. He has coached numerous skiers to become instructors and coaches, and he has helped very many pupils to change themselves from apprehensive intermediates to genuine black-run, and off-piste skiers. Including those over 65 & even 70. It can be done.

My thanks.

"…. let him not say that he knows better than his master, for he only holds a candle in sunshine"
William Blake.

My thanks

Skiing has been a major pleasure in my life. Teaching it, has been an even greater pleasure. My pupils have taught me more than I could ever have taught them, and I am grateful to you all. Seeing my pupils ski well is another pleasure, but it does not get close to the pleasure of seeing so many of you come to the important and joyful realisation that you are greater than you thought you were.

Not much compares with seeing someone "grow". Seeing them realise that they really did "have it in them" all along. Seeing you accepting that you can achieve things you never thought possible. Thank you, all of you. My only regret is that coaching is such an awful "business model" – my job is to help you be so successful that all too soon you no longer need me, and you disappear. Do at least stay in touch now and again.

Mostly (better get this in first) I need to thank Sue, my disproportionately generous, and tolerant wife of 53 years so far. But will it last? Without her willingness (eagerness ?) to see the back of me, season after season, I couldn't have done any of it.

I owe a sincere debt of gratitude to just a few, truly inspirational teachers, who were willing to put up with my quirks, my frustrations, my arrogance, my conceit, and my laboured learning.

In chronological order – thanks to Gerald Harrison, perhaps the best communicator I have ever encountered who opened my eyes to my own potential: he told me that I knew better than most that you can achieve anything you want. I have ruthlessly stolen huge chunks of his wisdom, but at least I give the credits when I do it, and spread the word. Thanks Gerald.

Thanks too, to Phil Smith. Few folk grin more than Phil on the slopes. He got me pushing my boundaries, and not kicking myself if it went wrong. He showed me that experimenting is more fun than perfect outcomes.

Hugh Monney taught me that trying too hard didn't work, but trying things out did, and how to trust my sub-conscious. He even convinced me that this very same sub-conscious learning works extremely well over long cups of coffee while the weather is bad outside – not that I took much convincing.

A very special thanks to a man I am honoured to call a friend, John Shedden. Creator of the English Ski Council. Founder member of the National Coaching Foundation. Founder member of B.A.S.I. (originally called BAPSI). Olympic selector. Erstwhile adviser to Franz Klammer, and genuinely England's "Mr.Skiing". I could go on. John has taught me more about the fundamentals of skiing than anyone else. His insistence on a robustly intellectual approach has I hope rubbed-off sufficiently for my own teaching to be true, and honest, intellectually rigorous and motivational.

Pascal Linden, friend and Chamonix Guide, has taken me to mountain places I would never have otherwise dared to go, and helped me be brave enough to get down them somehow or another, or at least kind enough to look away when it all went wrong. Once, watching me venture down a steep couloir he told me in his beautiful French accent, that the reason he stood *slightly* to one side was – "because it is better for one person to die, than two!"

Finally my thanks to Martin & Julia Webb of "spinningyourdreams.co.uk" for sorting out my hopeless photography, which almost sank this entire project.

Finally my thanks are due to a sizeable group of good skiing friends and pupils, too many to mention individually who have made planet Trueman a better place to live. To all the nay-sayers – you were wrong. To all the good folk out there, thank you. I hope we meet on slopes sometimes.

Bob Trueman.

Printed in Great Britain
by Amazon

36502729R00088